The
Workweek

This provocative book makes a compelling case for reducing the number of workdays in a week to four. Globalization has brought with it fiercer competition and greater worker mobility, and as organizations compete for top talent, they are becoming more open to unconventional worker arrangements, such as remote working and flextime.

International business expert, Robert Grosse, draws on scholarly research to construct an appealing argument for why the four-day workweek benefits both the organization and the employee. Research has demonstrated that longer work hours harm the individual and don't amount to a more effective organization, which begs the question: then why do it? The book goes beyond merely arguing that a reduced workweek is a good idea. It delves into why, explores the means for achieving it, and scrutinizes the barriers to getting there.

This is a book for forward-thinking executives, leaders, and academics who understand that work–life balance is the secret sauce not only for organizational success, but also for greater productivity and satisfaction in their careers and those of the people they manage.

Robert Grosse is Professor of Business Administration at Thunderbird School of Global Management, USA, and a former President of the Academy of International Business. He was the founding Director of Standard Bank Group's (South Africa) Global Leadership Centre and served as Dean of the School of Business Administration at American University of Sharjah, as well as the Director (Dean) of the EGADE Business School at Monterrey Tec in Mexico.

ROBERT GROSSE

The Four-Day
Workweek

Routledge
Taylor & Francis Group

NEW YORK AND LONDON

First published 2018
by Routledge
711 Third Avenue, New York, NY 10017

and by Routledge
2 Park Square, Milton Park, Abingdon, Oxon, OX14 4RN

Routledge is an imprint of the Taylor & Francis Group, an informa business

Library of Congress Cataloging-in-Publication Data
A catalog record for this book has been requested

ISBN: 978-1-138-05836-1 (hbk)
ISBN: 978-1-138-05838-5 (pbk)
ISBN: 978-1-315-16431-1 (ebk)

Typeset in Joanna MT
by Out of House Publishing

This book is dedicated to the next generation of the workforce, who hopefully will enjoy a four-day workweek – as well as other adjustments that add to the value of our work lives.

Contents

Contents

The concept of a four-day workweek has been around since the Second World War ended, once people's work returned to a normal basis. However, organized labor moved away from a focus on the length of the workweek to aim instead at other work conditions, particularly wages and benefits, health and safety conditions, and fair treatment of workers. And while organized labor has been greatly marginalized in the United States over this past half-century, no other group has taken the workweek issue as a target to pursue. This book aims to demonstrate why the four-day workweek is such a valuable goal to achieve today and how it could be pursued. At the end of the day, people should be allowed to work as many hours as they choose, but the standard should be a four-day week, given the level of economic development that has been achieved and the availability of machines and technology improvements that allow us to move forward from the 40-hour week established by Henry Ford in 1926.

Acknowledgments

I would like to thank a number of student assistants who helped in collecting the information used in this project. They include: Jose Villagomez, Sebastian Sierra, and Tarak Shahada. I would also like to thank three colleagues who read parts of this manuscript and offered valuable feedback as I was writing the book: Adrian Tschoegl, Rob Spich, and John Hume. And most importantly, I would like to thank my wife, Chris, for her willingness to let me hide in my office and click away at the chapters. Thank you all very much.

One

This book explores the possibility of moving the standard US work-week from its current level of 40 hours per week in five days to a new level of 32 hours per week in four days. The five-day, 40-hour week has been the standard in the US since Henry Ford launched this timetable at his company in 1926. On the face of it, a reduction to 32 hours seems like a preposterous suggestion given the current structure of employment and incomes earned by those working 40-hour weeks. However, even just looking at actual work hours during the past 50 years or so demonstrates that people are working somewhat fewer hours than previously – implying that the four-day workweek would be the continuation of a trend rather than a radical departure from historical practice. Regardless of one's preconceived ideas, it is worth a careful consideration of the pros and cons of the 32-hour week, along with the implications for the economy and for society.

THE BASIC PREMISE

Per capita incomes in the US went from an average $10,017 in 1925 to $52,195 in 2016 (both values in 2016 dollar terms). National income (gross domestic product [GDP]) in the US was $18.5 trillion in 2016. This is 18 times the current-dollar value of GDP in 1930, when John Maynard Keynes wrote that within 100 years he expected that people might be working 15-hour weeks (possibly in five days per week with three-hour workdays) because of the rapidly advancing production of goods and services worldwide at that time.[1] Perhaps this idea should be considered in more detail.

Clearly, one cannot look at these per capita income numbers and ignore that the cost of living has risen along with incomes; to have an income on the 1925 level today would put a person in the poverty category in the US. The logic here is not to say that income is unimportant today. Rather, it is to ask the question: with the incomes that we do have today, are we using our time to the best advantage? We should occasionally sit back and think about how we are using those 24 hours each day, or those 168 hours each week.

This is really a fundamental question of how we live our lives today. Do we want to devote more than half of our waking hours Monday to Friday at work, including getting there and back, and leave less than half for leisure and other activities? Why not reduce work time to 32 hours per week and leave 80 hours for other activities (assuming that we sleep eight hours/day × seven days/week = 56 hours per week)? If advances in technology and organization of work are improving productivity and increasing output all the time, why should we be working the same number of hours today as people worked when Henry Ford instituted the 40-hour workweek in 1926?[2]

From another perspective, rather than debating whether the automation of many jobs is reducing the demand for "traditional" labor in those activities that are automated, as discussed below[3] in Chapter 6, we should perhaps be thinking about how to use our time more beneficially. This may go against what people see as the work ethic – but the definition of that ethic needs to change along with the times. It is difficult to say that today, with a 40-hour workweek, people have less of a work ethic than in 1870, when the average workweek was over 60 hours. Or in other words, work is healthy; work generates income; work provides satisfaction – but work is not the whole story.

One of the goals of work is to provide for human needs; if our hard work and innovation allow us to reduce the time needed to produce goods and services, why shouldn't we use some of that extra time available to pursue non-work activities? After all, in the early 1800s, the average workweek in the US was about 70 hours/week. (See Appendix 1.1, which shows average workweeks in the US from 1830 until today.) That number dropped to about 60 hours per week after the Civil War, to 48 hours per week just after World War I, and to 40 hours per week in the late 1920s. Why not 32 hours now?

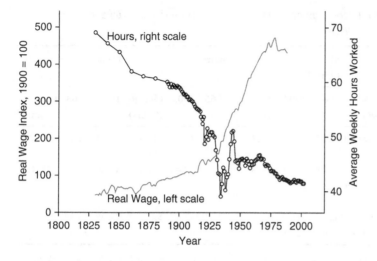

Figure 1.1 The Fall in the Market Workweek and the Gain in Real Wages
Source: Greenwood and Vandenbrouche (2005, p. 2).

Consider the trends over time of hours worked and income of people working in the US, as in Figure 1.1. Greenwood and Vandenbrouche (2005) reasoned that these trends occurred due to: (a) higher real incomes over time (leading to preference for more leisure time); (b) greater value of leisure time due to more and better leisure opportunities; and (c) reduced need for housework due to labor-saving devices. In fact, those authors attributed most of the reduction in work time to technological change that has both improved productivity and saved labor.

In a parallel vein, one could look at the amount of time used by people on work activities and other things, including leisure, sleep, housework, shopping, etc. Time use studies in the US (e.g., Aguiar and Hurst 2007), as described in Table 1.1, show that Americans between the ages of 21 and 65 spent an average of five hours more time on leisure activities in 2003 in comparison with their activities in 1965.[4] Men spent about six hours more of their days on leisure activities, while women spent four hours more; the women also replaced work at home with work in the marketplace extensively during this same time period. Men increased their leisure time largely by reducing primary work activity; women shifted some work from the home to the

Table 1.1 Unconditional Mean Levels of Time Use in 1965 and 2003 in Hours per Week

Time Use Category	All Individuals 1965	2003	Change (hours)	Males 1965	2003	Change (hours)	Females 1965	2003	Change (hours)
Total Market Work	35.98	31.71	−4.3	51.58	39.53	−12.1	22.45	24.93	2.5
Total Non-Market Work	22.09	18.31	−3.8	9.67	13.43	3.8	32.86	22.55	−10.3
Leisure	30.77	35.33	4.6	31.80	37.40	5.6	29.89	33.54	3.7
Sample Size	1,854	15,091		833	6,699		1,021	8,392	

Total hours in one week = 168; eight hours of sleep per day = 56 hours sleep per week. In 2003, people spent 85 hours on work plus leisure, so 27 hours per week were left for eating, personal care, child care, civic and religious activity, and education.

Source: Data from Aguiar and Hurst (2007, Tables 2 and 3).

office, but overall reduced the combined work activity and put more time into leisure activities.[5]

Note that the average male actually worked less than 40 hours per week in 2003 − and that the trend over these 40 years is clearly toward fewer market (job) work hours. Women, on the other hand, worked far less than 40 hours per week at market jobs, while they reduced their housework/childcare by more than ten hours per week. It would not be an unimaginable shift to drop the "total market work" week to 32 hours, since both men and women are advancing in the direction of such a target without any company or government policy in this regard anyhow.

This idea may appear particularly odd or difficult to grasp for white-collar or professional workers, who do not punch time clocks and who work hours that vary but that probably exceed 40 per week on average. How would these people adjust their work lives in this context? The answer is simple: they would have four workdays per week and three weekend days. The hours worked per day would not have to vary, and if employers really do move to a four-day week, then extra "make-up" hours would not be required during the longer weekend. The architect or banker, teacher or marketing manager would just have regular "office days" on four days per week, and then three days for relaxing, working at home, and/or pursuing other alternatives, including more market work if so desired.

For example, a management consultant would have four days in the week when he/she would be "at work," perhaps meeting with a client, doing research, developing solutions for the client, meeting with colleagues, etc. Then the three-day weekend would just replace the current two-day weekend. If this person is already working during some part of the existing two-day weekend, then he/she would likewise have to work for some part of the new three-day weekend. However, there presumably would be no client meetings or presentations or other interactions with the consulting firm's "market" during the three days off each week. This would logically lead to a lower number of hours spent on work per week by the consultant, even though the hours per day for the four workdays could remain well above the eight-hour blue-collar or office worker norm.

A teacher would have four class days per week and three weekend days. This would not eliminate the need to prepare materials and probably do some grading during the weekends, but it would not add to that burden. The challenge for teaching at, say, the elementary and secondary level will be to include enough class hours during the four weekdays to comply with government-established minimum class hours per week. If the "normal" school day includes 5.5 hours per day of instruction, then that implies $5.5 \times 5 = 27.5$ hours per week, not including breaks. This could be accomplished in four days with a seven-hour instructional day, but it would cut slightly into after-school activities and probably cause other complications that would have to be dealt with. Of course, the school year could be lengthened by a week or two to ensure that the typically required 990 annual instructional hours are met, but that adjustment would have its own complications, too.[6] This issue is discussed further in Chapter 7 below.

In contrast, an artist or a musician would still have performance dates and practice sessions that could be at any time, and thus would simply be outside the scope of the four-day week. Similarly, professional athletes would have games/competitions that would occur on some days, with practice sessions during many of the other days of the week, again outside of the scope of the four-day week. Writers such as the author of this book would also operate outside of the limits of the four-day week, though if they are also professors, they would have commitments to class and other university activities that would occur on the four workdays of the week.

The logic in favor of the four-day week is fundamentally based on the idea of a personal choice of time use among work, leisure, sleep, recreation, studies, and other possible activities. Given that in the 21st century there is no need to work just to obtain subsistence-level food, clothing, and shelter, the question is: how much time should be dedicated to work for income and how much should be allocated to other activities, including rest and leisure? Thus, the discussion should be focused on personal choices among alternatives such as additional work beyond the "normal" weekly hours, additional leisure activities, and additional time spent on other things such as education, health care, voluntary activities, and more. Once the newly established norm of working 32 hours per week is operating, then people can make these time-allocation decisions, just as they did when the workweek was reduced from 48 hours to 40 hours in the late 1920s.

If a person enjoys work and would prefer to use his/her time in that pursuit, then the four-day workweek would not preclude or penalize such activity.[7] If a person has various pursuits that he/she would like to carry out, then reducing the workweek to four days would open up more time for other pursuits, and thus presumably increase the person's satisfaction with the full set of activities chosen. In Chapter 4, we explore the revealed preferences of people in the US for their daily use of time in recent years, demonstrating that work is far from being the only priority for most people. Table 1.1 shows that people in the US have moved toward more leisure activities in the past 40 years, so the directional choice of time use is clear, even if people say in some surveys that they are motivated by greater income from increased work hours.

A major challenge to this move to a four-day workweek is the way that people "frame" their environment. A whole field of behavioral economics has developed in recent years looking at how people act under different conditions (and how those actions result in economic impacts), often being different from the anticipated actions based on expected utility theory. According to Tversky and Kahneman (1974), people tend to frame their views based on what they know and/or have experienced. So, if a person has never experienced a 32-hour, four-day workweek nor knows about it from observing others nor has learned about it from reading, then that person is likely to perceive the shorter workweek as an aberration from the "normal" 40-hour workweek and make judgments accordingly. The 32-hour workweek may very well bring greater satisfaction or well-being to the person than the 40-hour workweek, but he/she will not select it because of the framing bias based on experience. Tversky and Kahneman label this particular bias one of "anchoring"; that is, basing your view/ decision on previously observed situations that limits your ability to think objectively.

The allocation of time use presumably may differ across people and across cultures. For example, it turns out that in studies of people's preferences in the US and Europe, Europeans in general prefer more leisure time and Americans in general prefer more time at work and consequently more income (Okulicz-Kozaryn 2011).[8] As a result, we would expect Europeans to choose to "consume" much more of the extra time available with the four-day workweek in leisure activities, while Americans would presumably use more of that extra available time for additional work (e.g., either overtime or moonlighting at another job) and consuming less of it as leisure. Similar differences are likely between different groups of Americans as well. People in their 50s and 60s are more likely to prefer more leisure time than people in their 20s and 30s, based on their demonstrated preferences in recent years.

The underlying intent for this book is to demonstrate why a four-day workweek is desirable and how the reduced workweek will lead to better health and greater life satisfaction for people today. In a special issue of the *Journal of Business Ethics*, half a dozen authors explored the topic of "Working to Live or Living to Work?" As summarized by Burke (2009, p. 167), the set of authors found broadly that "Long work hours and work addiction harm individuals and their families and do not make organizations more effective."

One of the studies in this group is by Dembe (2009), who cites a number of research efforts that have shown that working overtime is associated with greater job-related injuries, psychological problems, disruption of family life, and worker dissatisfaction. Given this reality, the question of reducing work hours may be seen as an ethical issue, encouraging people to work fewer hours and thus to improve their health and well-being.

While the ethics focus is important, and it forms a conceptual basis for justifying the four-day workweek, this focus is too narrow. We also want to explore the choice between work and other activities, as well as the means through which the shorter workweek could be implemented, the relationships of the length of the workweek with additional topics such as productivity and motivation, and the implications of the shorter workweek for the production of leisure goods.

Finally, we do not want to get caught up in a debate on whether a reduced workweek would generate more employment to fill in (some of) the hours previously worked in the 40-hour workweek when the standard workweek becomes 32 hours. While it may seem obvious that taking 20% of weekly work away will require additional people to fill in the gap, this is far from assured. Of course, some people will continue to work 40-hour weeks anyway by choice. And some of the lost hours will be made up by increased hourly productivity of the less-burdened workers who only work 32 hours per week. Some additional hours are likely to be needed from someone to maintain existing output, at least in the short run. However, one result of reduced hours will be to push up wages, as a result of greater demand for workers. This will tend to decrease the demand for workers, and various studies have shown that the overall impact of a shorter workweek on employment is ambiguous (e.g., Kapteyn et al. 2004 for the US; Crepon and Kramarz 2002 for France; and Hunt 1999 for Germany). So, the logic of the analysis in this book is not based on generating additional employment but rather on generating additional choice for people's use of their time.

ORGANIZATION OF THE BOOK

In the next chapter, we consider quality of life and work hours, referring to literature on health vs. work hours and on happiness/satisfaction vs. work hours. Quality of life, as measured in a variety of ways, shows that job satisfaction, happiness, life satisfaction, and other indicators increase with fewer hours worked. This has been true over time in the US and across countries around the world. In all of the measures, the highest quality of life appears in the Nordic countries, plus Switzerland and The Netherlands, and similarly the lowest numbers of average hours worked per week occur in those same countries. The French government policy of requiring a 35-hour workweek for large employers since 2000 is also examined in this chapter.

In Chapter 3, the issues of worker motivation and worker productivity are explored in light of time spent at work, demonstrating an inverse correlation in both cases. Motivation as measured by employee job satisfaction and other indicators seems to be clearly greater when hours worked are fewer in the US and abroad, as well as over time. Productivity as measured by output per hour likewise is greater when hours worked per week are fewer. The chapter looks at a range of empirical examples, from the four-day, 40-hour compressed workweek that was implemented in quite a few companies in the 1970s and more recently, as well as in cases of 32-hour workweeks at several tech companies in recent years. While the compressed timetable of ten-hour days produced limited evidence of improved productivity and motivation, there were drawbacks noted, included greater fatigue during the four more-intense workdays. The limited examples of 32-hour workweeks provide tempting evidence of greater motivation and productivity – but the numbers of people involved are too few to be judged as a clear point of reference.

The question of what people would do with their newly available time is treated in Chapter 4, noting the impact on the production of leisure-related goods and services among other spillovers of the shorter workweek. Comparing weekday versus weekend time use in the US, it is found that people use their non-work time mostly for additional sleep and TV watching, although more time is also spent on housework, shopping, getting medical care, socializing, and participating in sports and recreation. So, it is expected that these activities will increase with the added weekend day, and the production of goods and services used in these activities will increase as well.

The main stumbling block to implementation of the four-day week is compensation of workers, and this subject is analyzed in terms of alternatives and means to smooth the transition period in Chapter 5. If work hours decrease by 20% under the 32-hour week, how do companies respond to this lost work? There is no complete answer, but it needs to be recognized that some of the reduced hours will be compensated by greater output per hour. The reduction in hours will also probably require hiring new people and having existing employees work some overtime initially, until productivity catches up with the output levels before the change. Who will absorb the costs involved? Chapter 5 evaluates various alternatives of companies, employees, and a combination of the two incurring the costs, along with various assumptions about changes in productivity. Government policy could be used as well through tax incentives to reduce the burden on individuals and on companies – though of course all taxpayers would eventually be impacted.

One theme that recurs every time the economy slows down and unemployment rises is the replacement of human work with machine work, so this topic is discussed as it complements the four-day workweek in Chapter 6. The Global Financial Crisis of 2008–9 was the most recent such phenomenon, and analysts questioned whether US unemployment would ever return to the sub-5% range (where it is again today). Machines clearly can replace humans in the workplace – but since the dawn of the industrial revolution and through the Internet age, more overall jobs have arisen in the economy alongside more machines. Chapter 6 traces technology changes and employment in the US over the past two centuries and notes the shift from an agricultural economy to a manufacturing and service economy to a largely service-based economy today. A number of studies are discussed in which expectations for future employment are presented, largely noting an expected reduction of opportunities in traditional manufacturing and growth in a wide range of services and some niche areas of manufacturing (e.g., biotechnology and materials science-based work).

The implementation of a four-day workweek will require adjustments to people's lives, incomes, and activities, so Chapter 7 looks at the implementation challenges in some detail. The main point is that one more day will need to be defined as part of the weekend – either Friday or Monday – and then work can be distributed accordingly. Businesses that operate longer hours already, such as restaurants, hotels, health care facilities, electric power facilities, etc., will not change their operations. However, they will need to find additional staffing, since the existing workforce will drop from 40 to 32 hours per week. This is mainly a scheduling problem, as discussed in Chapter 7. Since most likely only some organizations will shift to the 32-hour workweek initially, there will be a period of transition and various costs involved with some activities being on the four-day workweek and others still remaining on the old system.

A brief history of the workweek since the 1800s is discussed next in Chapter 8, showing the trend that is inexorably downward in hours per week, both in the US and around the world. Before the 1800s, most work was agricultural, and limited records exist concerning the workweek in those times. Evidence that does exist suggests that the workday was eight to nine hours long, six days per week, in the fields, with additional work done to operate the farm. When manufacturing and office work became dominant in the late 19th century, the workweek was still six days per week, with hours progressively moved to a ten-hour day. In the 20th century, further workweek reductions occurred, so that by the end of the Depression, US workweeks were largely 40 hours per week over five days. The workweek has not changed significantly since then, so part of our purpose is to argue that the trend should be continued toward fewer hours and days of work per week.

Chapter 9 considers the "future of work," which is quite a controversial topic due to the mechanization of many jobs, efforts to make worktime more flexible, the use of telecommuting, and other features of the modern workplace. Even if we went to a system in which people work predominantly at home or at a distance from the workplace, the four-day workweek would still be just as relevant. The idea of having a flexible schedule could complicate things if the flexibility crossed days rather than just shifting hours around during the day, but this is still quite manageable. An interesting discovery from searching the literature on future work conditions is that younger people today tend to have shorter tenure at a given company before switching jobs than older people – but this phenomenon has been true for the past 35 years or more! New work models such as Uber, Airbnb, and eBay are discussed, and it is noted that they constituted under 1% of employment in 2016.

Chapter 10 reflects the knee-jerk reaction that is common to this recommendation for moving to a four-day workweek: it is impossible! So that reaction needs to be defused. This chapter works through a number of the common arguments against the four-day workweek and demonstrates their lack of foundation in opposition to the proposed change. The first concern is: who will pay for the change? This issue is discussed in detail in Chapter 5, and here the discussion just highlights the ways in which costs and adjustments can be dealt with by companies, workers, and governments. Another argument is that the 40-hour workweek has always been the model, and that changing from it is not possible. Obviously, this is not true, on a historic basis as well as on a sociological basis, so some ideas are presented for dealing with the needed changes. The reasons why the 32-hour workweek will work are also discussed, emphasizing the fact that the workweek has been moving in this direction for at least half a century.

Finally, Chapter 11 offers some conclusions about how the four-day workweek can and is likely to be implemented and come caveats about the process. It also reviews some of the main findings of the previous chapters.

APPENDIX

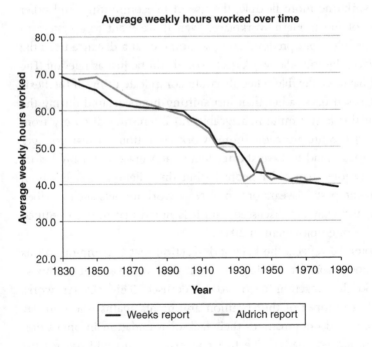

Figure A.1

Table A.1 Work Hours in the United States over Time Estimated Average Weekly Hours Worked in US Manufacturing, 1830–1990

Year	Weeks Report	Aldrich Report
1830	69.1	
1840	67.1	68.4
1850	65.5	69.0
1860	62.0	66.0
1870	61.1	63.0
1880	60.7	61.8
1890		60.0

Table A.2 Estimated Average Weekly Hours Worked in US, 1900–1988

Year	Census of Manufacturing	Jones Manufacturing	Owen Non-Student Males	Greis Manufacturing	Greis All Workers	Census All Workers
1900	59.6	55.0	58.5			
1904	57.9	53.6	57.1			
1909	56.8 (57.3)	53.1	55.7			
1914	55.1 (55.5)	50.1	54.0			
1919	50.8 (51.2)	46.1	50.0			
1924	51.1	48.8	48.8			
1929	50.6	48.0	48.7			
1934		34.4	40.6			
1940		37.6	42.5			43.3
1944		44.2	46.9			
1947		39.2	42.4	43.4	44.7	
1950		38.7	41.1			42.7
1953		38.6	41.5	43.2	44.0	
1958		37.8	40.9	42.0	43.4	
1960			41.0			40.9
1963			41.6	43.2	43.2	
1968			41.7	41.2	42.0	
1970			41.1			40.3
1973				40.6	41.0	
1978			41.3	39.7	39.1	
1980						39.8
1988						39.2

Source: Whaples, R. "Hours of Work in U.S. History", *Economic History Encyclopedia*, August 14, 2001.

http://eh.net/encyclopedia/hours-of-work-in-u-s-history/.

NOTES

1 Keynes also said that he expected that we may be eight times as well-off in terms of consumption of goods and services 100 years from the time of his writing. He also said that the main challenge in this environment may be to change the mentality that requires people to work in order to demonstrate their worth, rather than to enjoy the much higher standard of living that will be available. Much of this has come to pass in the 85 years since Keynes wrote these statements (see Keynes 1930).

2 See www.history.com/this-day-in-history/ford-factory-workers-get-40-hour-week.

3 See also www.technologyreview.com/featuredstory/515926/how-technology-is-destroying-jobs/.

4 The surveys include only households in which at least one person was employed during the previous year.

5 See, for example, Aguiar and Hurst (2007).

6 This 990-hour school year was the minimum allowed in New York, Virginia, Massachusetts, and more than 30 other states in 2016.

7 As one simple example, if a person who works in a five-day, 40-hour per week environment today is shifted to a four-day, 32-hour workweek under the new system, then that person should be permitted to work "overtime" to recoup the eight hours and income that were reduced – if he/she prefers to do so. Perhaps income could be reduced by only 10% to account for expected productivity gains from the shorter workweek. Compensation is a very important issue, and this is discussed in detail in Chapter 5.

8 Alesina et al. (2005) argue that Europeans work fewer hours per week than Americans primarily because of union policies and labor market regulations, rather than worker preferences. Prescott (2004) argues that it is due to higher tax rates in Europe.

REFERENCES

Aguiar, M. and E. Hurst (2007). "Measuring Trends in Leisure: The Allocation of Time over Five Decades". Quarterly Journal of Economics. Vol. 122, pp. 969–1006.

Alesina, A., E. Glaeser, and B. Sacerdote (2005). "Work and Leisure in the U.S. and Europe: Why So Different?", in NBER Macroeconomics Annual 2005, eds. M. Gertler and K. Rogoff. Cambridge, MA: MIT Press, pp. 1–64.

Burke, R. (2009). "Working to Live or Living to Work: Should Individuals and Organizations Care?" Journal of Business Ethics. Vol. 84, pp. 167–172.

Crepon, B. and F. Kramarz (2002). "Employed 40 Hours or Not Employed 39: Lessons from the 1982 Mandatory Reduction of the Workweek", Journal of Political Economy. Vol. 110, pp. 1355–1389.

Dembe, A. (2009), "Ethical Issues Relating to the Health Effects of Long Working Hours", Journal of Business Ethics. Vol. 84, pp.195–208.

Greenwood, J. and G. Vandenbroucke (2005). "Hours Worked: Long-run Trends". NBER Working Paper 11629. September. www.nber.org/papers/w11629.

Hunt, J. (1999). "Has Work-Sharing Worked in Germany?", *The Quarterly Journal of Economics*. Vol. 114, pp. 117–148.

Kapteyna, A., A. Kalwijb, and A. Zaidi (2004). "The Myth of Worksharing", *Labour Economics*. Vol. 11, pp. 293–313.

Keynes, J.M. (1930). "Economic Possibilities for our Grandchildren," in *Essays in Persuasion*. New York: Harcourt Brace, pp. 358–373.

Okulicz-Kozaryn, A. (2011), "Europeans Work to Live and Americans Live to Work (Who is Happy to Work More: Americans or Europeans?)", *Journal of Happiness Studies*. Vol. 12, pp. 225–243.

Prescott, E. (2004). "Why Do Americans Work So Much More Than Europeans?", *Federal Reserve Bank of Minneapolis Quarterly Review*. Vol. 28, pp. 2–14.

Tversky, A. and D. Kahneman (1974). "Judgment under Uncertainty: Heuristics and Biases". *Science*. Vol. 185, pp. 1124–1131.

Quality of Life and Satisfaction/Happiness
Two

One central issue in the discussion of a shorter workweek is whether or not this would lead to greater job satisfaction and/or quality of life. In this chapter, we explore the correlation of hours worked with worker satisfaction and with perceived quality of life. Our fundamental logic is that the four-day workweek is attractive because it opens up the individual's opportunity set for using their time in many more activities (or to remain with 40 hours of work, if desired). So, the change to a four-day workweek should increase worker satisfaction or happiness. It may consequently lead to a greater quality of life, including better health.

Before entering into that discussion a key question is raised: what is the goal of work? In short, do we work to live or live to work? This question is actually easy to answer – both directions are important, and individuals vary on their preferences between them. In any event, this question is examined in some detail before moving on to empirical evidence that broadly demonstrates greater satisfaction or happiness with fewer hours of work around the world and over time. The conclusion is that a 32-hour workweek is quite manageable as the baseline, as long as people are given the option to work longer hours if they choose.

THE GOAL OF WORK

The goal of work is to provide income for the individual/family that will enable them to live comfortably. This simple statement is true in the broad sense that a family must generate income adequate to live on, or suffer the fate of depending on a social welfare system in the US that is woefully inadequate.[1] Of course alternatives exist, such as support from other relatives or friends, and the definition of living comfortably is subject to great debate. But one key goal of working is to generate income sufficient for the needs of the family.

This discussion is not intended to resolve the question of how much income from work is adequate, but rather to move in the other direction and to note that the goal of work is actually multiple. Not only does work provide income, but it provides satisfaction to the worker, based on performance appraisals, co-worker interactions, and other socially reinforcing mechanisms. Work contributes to a person's sense of self-worth, and that is separable from the income generated. Work may also benefit the individual by providing a use of time that is entertaining; that is, an experience that in itself is enjoyable, perhaps because of the goals accomplished, the sense of power, the camaraderie, and/or the ability to pursue attractive goals. In sum, we could say that the goal of work is:

$$G_w = (\text{income for family} + \text{sense of self-worth} + \text{sense of power from work relationships} + \text{friendships} + \text{opportunity to do interesting things} + \text{other})$$

This statement is biased in the sense that the other elements beyond providing income for the family actually require the individual to have sufficient financial capability to provide for the family from some source, work or other. Once the fundamental need is satisfied, then the additional goals of work come into play. Think of a rural farmer in a less developed country or a person living in prehistoric times. In those cases, work was necessary for survival, and other attributes simply were not relevant or were of minor importance. Once societies developed and groups of people settled into towns and cities, the circumstances permitted differentiated jobs and division of labor. In modern times, the goal of work really is multiple, as described above.[2]

THE CORRELATION BETWEEN LESS WORK AND MORE SATISFACTION

Assuming that work has attraction beyond merely providing income, the next question is: how much work is "optimal" for an individual or family? To pursue this question, it is necessary to compare work with alternative uses of time. Would you prefer more work and more income, or less work and more time for the pursuit of other goals such as recreation, studies, doing things with the family, volunteering, etc.? This question is considered in Chapter 4 in terms of the revealed preferences of Americans for their time use. The current chapter looks at the relationship between hours worked and people's health, satisfaction, and other measures of well-being.

The correlation between hours worked and satisfaction has been approached from a variety of bases, such as relating measures of health to hours worked. For example, a meta-analysis of the relationship between hours of work and physical health showed a significant negative relationship between worker health and the number of hours worked (Sparks et al. 1997). Looking at workers in France after the imposition of the 35-hour workweek, Berniell (2014) showed that there was a significant drop in smoking and drinking and a significant increase in their physical activity when the workweek dropped from 39 to 35 hours. Another meta-analysis by Kivimaki et al. (2015) showed that longer work hours were associated with a greater risk of stroke.

A second perspective relates to quality of life. This quality can be measured in many ways; we begin with a measure of "happiness" as collected by the United Nations. This index measures happiness as a combination of income, life expectancy, lower corruption, freedom, social support, and generosity.[3] The United Nations' happiness report, with results from 2017 shown in Figure 2.1, ranks the Scandinavian countries and the Netherlands at the top of the list. The countries that have gone the farthest in reducing the workweek are these same countries. Table 2.1 shows average working hours per week in three dozen countries in 2016, with The Netherlands, Denmark, and Norway leading the list for the shortest workweeks.[4] In just about any survey of standard of living, job satisfaction, or happiness, these are the very countries that come out on top.

Looking at a range of 34 countries, the Organisation for Economic Co-operation and Development (OECD) Life Satisfaction Index, which compares member countries within that relatively wealthy group, still shows the northern European countries ahead of the US, and the US above most of the lower-income members in the OECD.

Note that this index covers only the "rich country" group of OECD members, but it does once again reinforce the relatively high ranking of the northern European countries, followed by the US and then southern and eastern Europe plus other dispersed OECD members.

Looking at eight European countries in 2007, Bäck-Wiklund et al. (2011) found that overall life satisfaction was highest in Sweden, The Netherlands, and Finland, and lowest in the UK, Hungary, and

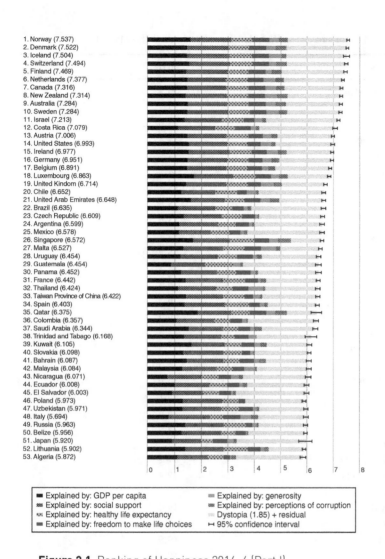

1. Norway (7.537)	
2. Denmark (7.522)	
3. Iceland (7.504)	
4. Switzerland (7.494)	
5. Finland (7.469)	
6. Netherlands (7.377)	
7. Canada (7.316)	
8. New Zealand (7.314)	
9. Australia (7.284)	
10. Sweden (7.284)	
11. Israel (7.213)	
12. Costa Rica (7.079)	
13. Austria (7.006)	
14. United States (6.993)	
15. Ireland (6.977)	
16. Germany (6.951)	
17. Belgium (6.891)	
18. Luxembourg (6.863)	
19. United Kindom (6.714)	
20. Chile (6.652)	
21. United Arab Emirates (6.648)	
22. Brazil (6.635)	
23. Czech Republic (6.609)	
24. Argentina (6.599)	
25. Mexico (6.578)	
26. Singapore (6.572)	
27. Malta (6.527)	
28. Uruguay (6.454)	
29. Guatemala (6.454)	
30. Panama (6.452)	
31. France (6.442)	
32. Thailand (6.424)	
33. Taiwan Province of China (6.422)	
34. Spain (6.403)	
35. Qatar (6.375)	
36. Colombia (6.357)	
37. Saudi Arabia (6.344)	
38. Trinidad and Tabago (6.168)	
39. Kuwait (6.105)	
40. Slovakia (6.098)	
41. Bahrain (6.087)	
42. Malaysia (6.084)	
43. Nicaragua (6.071)	
44. Ecuador (6.008)	
45. El Salvador (6.003)	
46. Poland (5.973)	
47. Uzbekistan (5.971)	
48. Italy (5.694)	
49. Russia (5.963)	
50. Belize (5.956)	
51. Japan (5.920)	
52. Lithuania (5.902)	
53. Algeria (5.872)	

- ■ Explained by: GDP per capita
- ▧ Explained by: social support
- ▨ Explained by: healthy life expectancy
- ■ Explained by: freedom to make life choices
- ▨ Explained by: generosity
- ▨ Explained by: perceptions of corruption
- ▨ Dystopia (1.85) + residual
- ⊢⊣ 95% confidence interval

Figure 2.1 Ranking of Happiness 2014–6 (Part I)

Source: http://worldhappiness.report/wp-content/uploads/sites/2/2017/03/HR17.
pdf.

Bulgaria. Their survey covered a total of 7,867 employees in four
sectors in each country: banks or insurance companies, retail companies, telephone companies, and hospitals. Their country ranking
of overall life satisfaction looks very similar to the others above, and
correlates highly negatively with the number of hours worked per
week in each country.

Table 2.1 Average Usual Weekly Hours Worked on the Main Job

Country	2016
The Netherlands	29.1
Denmark	32.1
Norway	34.0
Switzerland	34.4
Germany	34.5
Ireland	34.7
Belgium	35.2
Italy	35.5
Austria	35.6
Australia	35.7
Sweden	35.9
France	36.1
Finland	36.2
United Kingdom	36.5
Spain	36.5
Luxembourg	37.3
New Zealand	37.4
Estonia	38.3
United States	38.6
Canada	38.7
Iceland	38.8
Greece	39.0
Slovenia	39.2
Slovak Republic	39.2
Czech Republic	39.4
Brazil	39.4
Portugal	39.4
Hungary	39.6
Poland	39.9
Israel	40.6
South Africa	43.1
Chile	43.4
Korea	43.8
Mexico	45.2
Turkey	47.9

Source: OECD Statistical Abstracts, 2017. https://stats.oecd.org/Index.
aspx?DataSetCode=ANHRS.

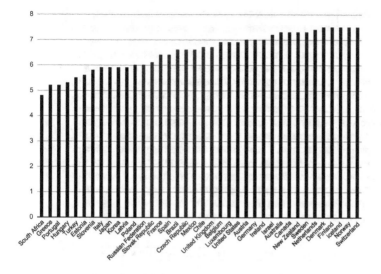

Figure 2.2 OECD Life Satisfaction Index 2015
Source: www.oecdbetterlifeindex.org/topics/life-satisfaction/.

And finally, looking at a measure of employee satisfaction (see Figure 2.3), the Randstad Workmonitor survey[5] showed the following ranking of 32 diverse countries in 2017 (only the top 16 are shown in the figure). Interestingly, Mexico, India, and the US ranked on top in this survey, while once again, the Scandinavian and northern European countries filled out the other highest-ranked countries for satisfied workers in this global comparison of 32 countries.

In another study, Collewet and Loog (2015) found that, in Germany, an additional hour of work in the workweek decreased life satisfaction significantly for men and insignificantly for women. Apparently, there is a positive impact on life satisfaction when the workweek is reduced. Since the countries in Table 2.1 also have very high per capita incomes in relation to the rest of the world, it seems that incomes do not have to suffer either when the workweek is shorter.

A NOTE ON HAPPINESS

While the above discussion cited "happiness" as one measure of satisfaction of workers in the US and other countries, the meaning of "happiness" is not at all clear. According to one statement, we could define happiness by saying that "it includes the experience of joy,

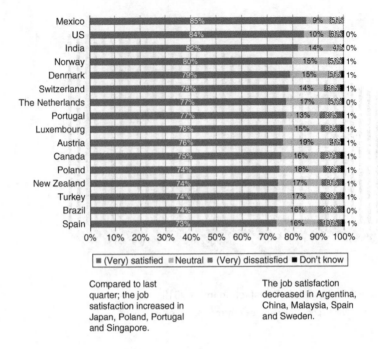

	(Very) satisfied	Neutral	(Very) dissatisfied	Don't know
Mexico	85%	9%	5%	
US	84%	10%	6%	0%
India	82%	14%	4%	0%
Norway	80%	15%	5%	1%
Denmark	79%	15%	5%	1%
Switzerland	78%	14%	6%	1%
The Netherlands	77%	17%	5%	0%
Portugal	77%	13%	9%	1%
Luxembourg	76%	15%	8%	1%
Austria	76%	19%	4%	1%
Canada	75%	16%	8%	1%
Poland	74%	18%	7%	1%
New Zealand	74%	17%	8%	1%
Turkey	74%	17%	9%	1%
Brazil	74%	16%	10%	0%
Spain	73%	16%	10%	1%

Compared to last quarter; the job satisfaction increased in Japan, Poland, Portugal and Singapore.

The job satisfaction decreased in Argentina, China, Malaysia, Spain and Sweden.

Figure 2.3 Randstad Job Satisfaction Index

Source: Randstad Workmonitor, Q1 March 2017. p. 34. https://cdn2.hubspot.net/hubfs/481927/Campaigns/Randstad%20Workmonitor_Global_Q1_March2017%20(1).pdf?submissionGuid=21acc38a-c78f-407a-a65b-1e0e6a00cae6.

contentment, or positive well-being, combined with a sense that one's life is good, meaningful, and worthwhile" (Lyubomirsky 2001, p. 239). While this statement seems simple enough, the measure of happiness of one person versus another may not correlate with greater work motivation or performance.

A number of studies have questioned whether happier workers are indeed more productive (e.g., Silvestro 2002; van Kleef et al. 2004; Cederström and Spicer 2015). A review of the literature on the subject of happiness and work performance (Fisher 2010) showed that most studies have indeed supported the relationship between happiness or job satisfaction and performance, especially productivity. Even so, the definition of happiness may focus more on personal satisfaction or on altruistic beliefs (hedonic vs. eudaimonic), and the implications for productivity differ. While is it important to raise this issue, our conclusions will remain based on the vast majority of findings

of a positive correlation between happiness or satisfaction and job performance.

THE FRENCH 35-HOUR WORKWEEK

France implemented a 35-hour workweek in legislation passed in 1998, taking effect in 2000. This law required companies to limit hourly workers to a "normal" 35 hours per week, allowing overtime paid at 50% more, for a maximum of 48 total hours per week.[6] Managerial employees initially were not regulated, and subsequently were limited to 218 working days per year, which was later increased to 235 days per year (cf. Lehndorff 2014). This law was passed by a socialist government that wanted to use it to expand employment in France, where the unemployment rate had been well above 10% of the labor force for several years.

De facto, hours worked by hourly workers in France initially declined by one to two hours per week in 2001–2 from an initial average of 39.6 hours per week in 1999, and then returned to about 39 hours per week after 2002 (Lehndorff 2014, p. 846). That is, while the law stipulated 35 hours as the workweek and people initially dropped their weekly hours toward that target, they ultimately chose to work overtime to maintain approximately 39 hours/ week as the average. And managerial employees were found to have no change in their actual work hours per week under the policy. This finding from 2014 needs to be revisited, since, as is shown in Table 2.1, French workers dropped their de facto workweek to 36.1 hours in 2016.

The empirical result of this policy in terms of productivity, worker satisfaction, unemployment, and other measures of performance is insignificant. That is, measures of productivity and worker satisfaction in France during 2000–15 do not show a clear impact of the policy, and French unemployment during the period has ranged from 10.2% in 2000 to 11.0% in 2014. Figure 2.4 shows these measures over the 15-year period.

The correlations among these three variables are very low. Unemployment and worker productivity have a Pearson correlation coefficient of 0.10, while life satisfaction is only correlated with productivity growth at −0.23.[7] Neither of these values is statistically significant.

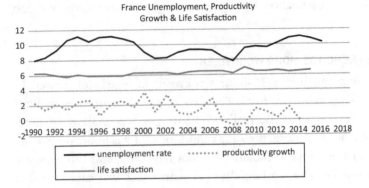

France Unemployment, Productivity
Growth & Life Satisfaction

Figure 2.4 French Productivity Growth, Worker Satisfaction, and Unemployment During 2000–15

Values in % per year; satisfaction is a decimal value

Sources: http://stats.oecd.org/Index.aspx?DatasetCode=LEVEL; https://knoema.com/IMFWEO2017Apr/imf-world-economic-outlook-weo-database-april-2017; www.randstad.com/press/research-reports/research-reports/.

The French policy may have some useful implications for US policy. First of all, the fact that people initially only dropped their work hours by at most two hours per week from their previous level implies that employees wanted to maintain or increase their incomes and were willing to work the hours needed to achieve that goal. Second, the fact that by 2016, even without new legislation, the French average workweek had declined to 36.1 hours implies that the social change needed to implement lower work hours has indeed taken hold after one and a half decades. If the US wants to achieve a shorter workweek more quickly, it may be more successful by dropping a workday than by shortening the number of hours per workday.

The French policy is difficult to evaluate in a conclusive manner, since so many things varied at the same time: minimum working hours were reduced without reducing weekly wages; companies received fiscal benefits to partially offset the higher labor costs; managerial workers were largely unaffected by the 35-hour rule; not all companies and employers were subject to the rules; the rules were implemented in stages and later conservative governments encouraged longer working hours, though they did not eliminate the 35-hour rule; and finally, unemployment was quite high in France during the entire period of 1998–2015, so it is difficult to say that the policy worked in terms of reducing unemployment.[8]

One study (Berniell 2014) found that the 35-hour workweek led initially to reduced alcohol and tobacco consumption by workers and increased physical activity. This study compared workers' characteristics in 1998 and 2002 as before/after results. For this short period of time, the reduction in work hours seems to have produced an improvement in the health of French workers – ignoring the many other factors occurring at that time.

DIFFERENCES BETWEEN THE US AND EUROPEAN COUNTRIES

It is quite clear from Table 2.1 that workweek hours in the US are higher than in most countries of northern Europe and lower than in most countries of Eastern Europe and other emerging markets. With respect to the happiness indicator, it appears that the US also ranks lower than most of northern Europe and above most of Eastern Europe and other emerging markets. This is, however, just a snapshot of the relationship between working time and happiness. Surprisingly, the workweek difference is not a long-term cultural phenomenon – in the US and European countries, work hours were quite similar as recently as 1970, as shown in Figure 2.5. In the intervening years, European countries have cut the workweek far more rapidly than the US.

Alesina et al. (2005) argue that the reasons for the recent decline in European versus US hours worked have more to do with greater unionization and greater labor regulation in Europe than in the US, as against the possibility of innate cultural differences. Prescott (2004) makes an alternative argument that higher taxes in Europe make it less attractive to work more and earn higher incomes there. So, the incentive to use relatively more time in leisure exists in Europe in recent years. Another argument is that workers have less job security in the US than in Europe, and so they feel more compelled to work long hours to protect their livelihoods.[9]

The full set of reasons may be quite large, and our main interest is just to note that the US and European countries today have notably different workweeks, with Americans spending more time on the job (and more weeks on the job, as well as taking fewer vacations). And at the same time, the happiness index, as well as other measures of job

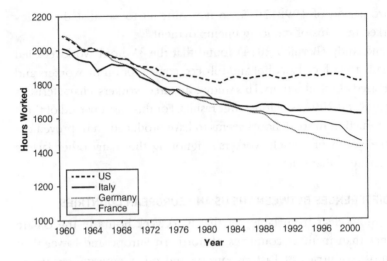

Figure 2.5 Annual Hours Worked over Time

Source: Alesina et al. (2005, p. 2). Originally from OECD data, annual hours per employed person. Annual hours are equivalent to 52 × usual weekly hours minus holidays, vacations, and sick leave.

and life satisfaction, seem to favor the northern European countries relative to the US.

HAPPINESS AND INCOME

Our discussion has focused on the relationship between happiness and hours worked during the week. Another clearly related issue is the correlation between happiness and income. In the economics literature, Richard Easterlin (1974; 1995) found that, in the US and a dozen other countries, people's real incomes increased over time, but their happiness did not. He initially attributed this to the idea that people view their happiness as related to their own incomes and the incomes of other people, so that as everyone's income increased over time, an individual would not feel happier, since his/her position did not change relative to others. Even so, at any given time, people with higher incomes tended to perceive greater happiness than people with lower incomes.

Another issue raised by Kahneman and Krueger (2006) is that people's responses to questions about their happiness/satisfaction are inconsistent over time. People offer higher evaluations of their life happiness when they are in a good mood or when they are healthier. People offer more extreme evaluations of their happiness immediately after events such as injuries (negative), successes (positive), illnesses (negative), marriage (positive), etc. People do not give higher evaluations as their income rises over time. But they do rate themselves happier when their incomes rise relative to those of other people they know.

These various elements point out that any happiness index will have weaknesses depending on the intended use of the measure. This brief section has discussed the relationship between happiness and personal income. Our overall interest is fairly simple in that we just want to know if people's happiness rises with fewer hours/days of work in the week. In the short run, this is likely to be correlated with income, since an abrupt drop in hours worked would probably be accompanied by some decrease in personal income. But this would be overcome over time as incomes return to the path of increase due to productivity increases. In our context of hours worked versus happiness, it seems that the key is what people would do with extra hours available for a choice of activities when the workweek is reduced.

LET PEOPLE CHOOSE – BUT ESTABLISH A 32-HOUR, FOUR-DAY BASELINE

Although we could use the lower workweek hours in Europe as an argument for reducing US hours, the logic is really in favor of choice. If we move to a four-day workweek in the US, then people will be able to choose between more (or the same) work versus more use of their time for other activities. It is easy to see that with more choices people will be better off, regardless of whether they choose to use greater time on more work or on other activities.

The challenge is to get to the 32-hour workweek from where we are today. Chapter 7 explores this challenge in some detail. For the moment, it is useful to recognize that inertia really exists, and that moving away from a 40-hour workweek, which has been established as the workweek for the past three generations of people, is quite a task. As much as one can argue that more choice for deciding how to use your time is more desirable, still the psychological barrier to making a shift away from work to other activities for those eight hours is enormous. As discussed widely in the literatures of behavioral economics and behavioral finance, once people get a certain frame of reference as being "permanent," it is extremely difficult to get them to change that perspective (e.g., Tversky and Kahneman 1974). That is, they "anchor" themselves to that reality as being the normal state of affairs and have trouble seeing alternatives.[10]

It may turn out that people choose to reassign their time only once the 32-hour workweek becomes the baseline for work. This adjustment is considered in Chapter 4. As long as the choices of some people will be to use the freed-up eight hours per week in some non-work activity(ies), then the positive impact of the four-day workweek is assured. That is, in the Pareto optimal sense, some people will be better off as they reassign part of their week to other activities and other people will be no worse off if they continue to work for 40 hours per week.

NOTES

1 See, for example, Bruch, http://journalistsresource.org/studies/government/congress/inequalities-safety-net-programs-poor.

2 In a perhaps trivial manner, one could assert that the goals of work should be weighted according to importance, and in early times the weight of providing for family needs was essentially 100% of the total. Nowadays, the weights are distributed across income, satisfaction, and other attributes.

3 A key missing element to the happiness measures presented here is the comparative position of the person on the income scale. If a person is higher than peers with whom he/she interacts, then happiness tends to be higher, *ceteris paribus*. See, for example, Kahneman and Krueger (2006).

4 A simple Spearman rank correlation between the top 20 countries in happiness and the 20 countries with the lowest hours worked per week is −0.63 − a strong 63% negative correlation between perceived happiness and greater number of hours worked.

5 The Randmonitor appears in www.randstad.com/press/research-reports/.

6 The reduction in weekly hours from 39 to 35 under the new law called for no change in worker compensation. Thus, companies had to suffer a 10% reduction in hours per week at the same wage level. This was partially balanced by fiscal incentives offered by the French government. See Askenazy (2013) for more details.

7 Data on worker satisfaction were only available for 2011–4, whereas life satisfaction data go back to 1990. Both curves were essentially flat.

8 It is true that hours worked declined in 2000 and 2001 and that unemployment declined in both of those years well. The causality is complicated because those were the last years of the global economic boom that was shocked by the 9/11

attacks at the end of 2001 and the slower growth that followed for a couple of years, before the huge slowdown cause by the Global Financial Crisis starting in 2008. It is always difficult to separate out causal relationships in the macro-economy, since so many things vary at once.

9 Ciulla (2001) makes the case that workers in the US feel job-related pressure to work long hours, and they are misled in doing so because employers tend not to be loyal to the workers. When times are difficult or when the company changes direction, they may be laid off despite commitment to the company.

10 This phenomenon might better be classified as Tversky and Kahneman's idea of "*availability*," meaning that people come to expect the 40-hour workweek as the permanent state of the world because that is the only reference they have available to them. I prefer the idea of "*anchoring*" because once people have their views anchored in a given reality, it is very difficult to pull up the anchor and move.

REFERENCES

Alesina, A., E. Glaeser, and B. Sacerdote (2005). "Work and Leisure in the United States and Europe: Why So Different?", in NBER Macroeconomics Annual 2005. Vol. 20, eds. M. Gertler and K. Rogoff. Cambridge, MA: MIT Press, pp. 1–64.

Askenazy, P. (2013). "Working time regulation in France from 1996 to 2012", Cambridge Journal of Economics. Vol. 37, pp. 323–347.

Bäck-Wiklund, M., T. van der Lippe, L. den Dulk, and A. Doorne-Huiskes (Eds.) (2011). Quality of Life and Work in Europe: Theory, Practice and Policy. London: Palgrave Macmillan.

Berniell, I. (2014). "The Effect of Working Hours on Health", http://ftp.iza.org/dp10524.pdf.

Bruch, S. (2015). "Inequalities in U.S. 'safety net' programs for the poor", https://journalistsresource.org/studies/government/congress/inequalities-safety-net-programs-poor.

Cederström, C. and A. Spicer (2015). The Wellness Syndrome. New York: Wiley.

Ciulla, J. (2001). The Working Life: The Promise and Betrayal of Modern Work. New York: Crown Business.

Coad, A. and M. Blinder (2014). "Causal Linkages between Work and Life Satisfaction and Their Determinants in a Structural VAR Approach", Working Paper #809, Levy Economics Institute of Bard College. June, www.levyinstitute.org/pubs/wp_809.pdf.

Collewet, M. and B. Loog (2015). "The Effect of Weekly Working Hours on Life Satisfaction", www.iza.org/conference_files/SUMS_2015/collewet_m21737.pdf.

Easterlin, R.A. (1974). "Does Economic Growth Improve the Human Lot? Some Empirical Evidence", in Nations and Households in Economic Growth: Essays in Honor of Moses Abramovitz, eds. R. David and M. Reder. New York: Academic Press, pp. 89–125.

Easterlin, R. (1995). "Will Raising the Incomes of All Increase the Happiness of All?", Journal of Economic Behavior and Organization. Vol. 27, pp. 35–47.

Epstein, B. and M. Kimball (2014). "The Decline of Drudgery and the Paradox of Hard Work", International Finance Discussion Papers #1106. Board of Governors of the

Federal Reserve System. June, www.federalreserve.gov/pubs/ifdp/2014/1106/ifdp1106.pdf.

Fisher, C.D. (2010) "Happiness at work", International Journal of Management Reviews. Vol. 12, pp. 384–412.

Kahneman, D. and A. Krueger (2006). "Developments in the Measurement of Subjective Well-Being", Journal of Economic Perspectives. Vol. 20, pp. 3–24.

Kivimaki, M., et al. (2015), "Long Working Hours and Risk of Coronary Heart Disease and Stroke: A Systematic Review and Meta-Analysis of Published and Unpublished Data for 603,838 Individuals", The Lancet. Vol, 386, pp. 1739–1746.

Lehndorff, S. (2014). "It's a Long Way from Norms to Normality: The 35-Hour Week in France", Industrial & Labor Relations Review. Vol. 67, pp. 838–863.

Lyubomirsky, S. (2001). "Why Are Some People Happier Than Others?", American Psychologist. Vol. 56, pp. 239–249.

Okulicz-Kozaryn, A. (2011). "Europeans Work To Live and Americans Live To Work", Journal of Happiness Studies. Vol. 12, pp. 225–243.

Prescott, E. (2004). "Why Do Americans Work So Much More Than Europeans?", Federal Reserve Bank of Minneapolis Quarterly Review. Vol. 28, pp. 2–14.

Silvestro, R. (2002) "Dispelling the modern myth: Employee satisfaction and loyalty drive service profitability", International Journal of Operations & Production Management. Vol. 22, pp. 30–49.

Sparks, K., C. Cooper, Y. Fried, and A. Shirom (1997). "The effect of hours of work on health: a meta-analytic review", Journal of Occupational and Organizational Psychology. Vol. 70. pp. 391–408.

Tversky, A. and D. Kahneman (1974). "Judgment under Uncertainty: Heuristics and Biases", Science. Vol. 185, pp. 1124–1131.

United Nations (2017). World Happiness Report. New York: United Nations, http://worldhappiness.report/wp-content/uploads/sites/2/2017/03/HR17.pdf.

van Kleef, G.A., C.K.W. De Dreu, and A.S.R. Manstead (2004). "The Interpersonal Effects of Anger and Happiness in Negotiations". Journal of Personality and Social Psychology. Vol. 86, pp. 57–76.

Three

How will a 32-hour workweek affect the motivation and productivity of the workforce? The results should be positive for motivation, since workers will have more time for leisure and other activities.[1] Whether this translates into greater productivity during the day is a question that is more difficult to answer, although experiments with a compressed four-day, 40-hour workweek in the 1970s did provide some evidence in this regard. And several small-scale examples exist in which companies or jurisdictions tried out shorter workweeks, offering some results to examine. Also, the large-scale example of France with its government-mandated 35-hour workweek – although that did not use the four-day model – has produced a large amount of discussion and evaluation, as presented in Chapter 2.

Before exploring the relationship of the workweek with motivation and productivity, it may be worth reflecting on the relationship between motivation and productivity. It stands to reason, for example, that happier workers should be more motivated and that they should therefore be more productive. It is probably best not to try to define happiness[2] or to pursue the line of reasoning that "happy workers are productive workers," since the definition of happiness is not clear in its application to business. One definition is that a happy person is "someone who experiences frequent positive emotions, such as joy, interest, and pride, and infrequent (though not absent) negative emotions, such as sadness, anxiety and anger" (Lyubomirsky et al. 2005, p. 115). While this may be a reasonable definition of happiness, it does not translate into behavior that would necessarily be positive or negative for business. So, we will look more narrowly at the relationship between motivation (or job satisfaction) and productivity here.

A number of studies have explored this relationship between motivation and productivity. Harter et al. (2002) used a large set of Gallup polls of people in companies and found that productivity was strongly positively correlated with job satisfaction and employee engagement. Grant (2008) explored the relationship between pro-social motivation (i.e., the desire to benefit other people) and productivity and also found a strong positive correlation. Ng et al. (2004) looked at factors that demotivated workers and led to reduced productivity in a construction context. They found that materials availability, overcrowded work areas, and need for rework were the primary demotivating factors that reduced productivity. Silvestro (2002) paradoxically found that supermarket employees performed worse when they were more satisfied and better when they were less satisfied.[3]

This chapter proceeds by reviewing the evidence concerning motivation, based on studies of the compressed four-day, 40-hour workweek. Then studies are considered with respect to the question of employee productivity. This is followed by an examination of other shorter workweek models, including the ones in France and Sweden, and a few individual company examples. There are very few examples of the 32-hour, four-day workweek that is the goal of this book, so it is not really possible to draw strong conclusions about this model based only on historical examples.

MOTIVATION IN EXPERIMENTS WITH A FOUR-DAY, 40-HOUR COMPRESSED WORKWEEK

Although the concepts are not identical, motivation of people to work has generally been measured in terms of job satisfaction, life satisfaction, or some other measure of perceived enjoyment of work conditions. For the purpose of our discussion, satisfaction will be used to imply motivation of the workers involved in the various workweek alternatives.

Ronen and Primps (1981) reviewed more than a dozen studies of a compressed workweek during the 1970s. They found that in most of the studies, workers claimed greater job satisfaction once the four-day workweek was implemented. Almost all of these studies were one-time snapshots of worker satisfaction and productivity. Two of those studies looked at satisfaction over time. One of those found that workers responded less favorably when surveyed after one year of operation of the four-day, 40-hour workweek policy. And after two years of time under the four-day workweek policy, they responded to eight out of nine questions that they were not more motivated or more satisfied than before it was implemented (Ivancevich and Lyon

1977). The other longitudinal study (Nord and Costigan 1973) found that 81% of the 200 employees in the survey were highly favorable to the change, though over time the level of satisfaction diminished slightly out to one year after the new policy was implemented.

Among the studies looking at worker job satisfaction after the implementation of a four-day, 40-hour workweek, Hodge and Tellier (1975) surveyed 223 people in 12 companies across the US and found overwhelming evidence that job satisfaction was significantly increased. This outcome applied across categories of age, gender, education, salary, and other demographics. The authors note that by far the most important contributing factor to greater job satisfaction was greater leisure time and the ability to organize leisure activities better with the extra weekend day. Negative factors included greater fatigue and general dislike of the longer workday.

Steele and Poor (1970) surveyed 148 workers and 20 managers at thirteen companies, finding that 46% of employees liked their company more, 49% had no change, and 5% liked their company less with the implementation of the four-day workweek. Of 44 people responding to a question about why they joined the firm in question, 77% said that the four-day week was the main attraction, and the rest said that it was not a factor – no one viewed it as a negative factor. A total of 14% of the workers said that fatigue was a negative aspect of the longer workdays in the four-day workweek. Almost all of the respondents said that greater opportunity for leisure activities was a major plus for the program. Overall, 96% of the male employees and 92% of the female employees were "pleased" or "very pleased" with the four-day compressed workweek.

Goodale and Aagaard (1975) found broad agreement among 474 employees of the accounting division in a multinational firm studied in 1972, a year after the four-day compressed workweek was instituted. A total of 65% of the respondents felt that they had more leisure time and about the same percentage felt that the switch to the four-day workweek was a positive change overall; 78% of the 474 people in this study did not want to return to the traditional five-day workweek.[4] Interestingly, younger workers were significantly more positive about the four-day workweek than older workers; workers were more positive than managers and supervisors; and lower-income people were more positive than higher-income people in the company.

Poor (1970) studied 27 companies that had implemented a four-day workweek in 1970 and found that workers had higher morale (86% of the firms) and lower absenteeism (85% of the firms) and the companies were more successful in recruitment (86% of the firms). There is no question that the overall response in these surveys was that job satisfaction did improve, to a lesser or greater degree.

Bird (2010) cites a number of additional 1970s studies that found that employee satisfaction diminished over time as the four-day, 40-hour workweek continued. The level of satisfaction was never lower than before the implementation of the compressed four-day work-week, but it was generally less strongly positive than just after implementation. In light of the fact that the compressed workweek did not take off after the initial period of interest, Bird suggests that perhaps there was a "Hawthorne effect" in which employees and employers alike (not to speak of authors!) were positively inclined to the new work arrangement because of its newness, which then wore off over time.

Almost 40 years later, in 2008, the State of Utah Government moved to a four-day, 40-hour workweek for most of the State's 25,000 employees.[5] This project was launched by Governor Huntsman as a means of reducing state expenditures on electricity and gasoline use, as well as to improve services to residents and provide a more attractive work environment for employees. A study of the impact of this policy on workers (Facer and Wadsworth 2010) nine months after implementation showed that 82% of them preferred to stay on the four-day, 40-hour schedule. The policy was ended in September of 2011, after the government had determined that the cost savings were not as significant as originally forecasted, and some residents had complained about reduced services due to Friday closing of state offices.

PRODUCTIVITY IN EXPERIMENTS WITH A COMPRESSED FOUR-DAY, 40-HOUR WORKWEEK

Among the studies reviewed by Ronen and Primps (1981), most reported a significant increase in worker productivity, while several also noted the feeling of greater fatigue among those employees. Ivancevich (1974) found exactly these outcomes, with supervisors noting a significant increase in the rate of production and overall output, along with half of workers reporting greater fatigue. Steele and Poor (1970) found that most of 13 companies studied reported greater output, with 14% of employees reporting greater fatigue.

Poor (1970) found that 27 companies that had switched to the four-day, 40-hour workweek all had lower costs as a result, 73% had higher profits, and two-thirds had higher output. In contrast, Calvasina and Boxx (1975) found no increase in productivity in two plants of the same manufacturing company after the four-day, 40-hour workweek was implemented. Calvasina and Boxx pointed out that their findings may support the compressed workweek, because they found that the change did not *decrease* productivity! And if other studies showing increased worker satisfaction are conclusive, then this would be supportive of the four-day compressed workweek.

Wheeler et al. (1972) surveyed managers in 143 US companies that had implemented a four-day, 40-hour workweek and found that 38% experienced a decrease in operating costs, while 11% incurred higher costs using this format. A total of 62% of these companies experienced an increase in overall production, while 3% showed a decline. The managers responded that efficiency had increased in 66% of the companies, while it decreased in 3% of them. Across all of these measures, it appears that productivity rose with the compressed four-day workweek in most companies.[6]

The State of Utah program in 2008 did not measure worker productivity directly, but it did survey users of the state government's services. Nine months after the program was initiated, 66% of respondents to a survey said that the four-day, 40-hour workweek should be continued and 20% said that it should be ended. The main complaints were about a lack of Friday services, even though some services such as driver's licensing had been extended to Fridays based on consumer feedback. When it dropped the program in 2011, the government cited the fact that measurement of economic benefits from the program showed very little reduction in electricity use or driving by state employees; the overall cost savings of the program were negligible.[7]

These studies focused on a compressed workweek, packing 40 hours into four days instead of five. The goal of the four-day workweek in the present discussion is to reduce hours worked and to permit greater leisure time. This approach was not tested in the 1970s analyses, nor in the 2000s cases such as the State of Utah example. Direct measures of the benefits and costs of a 32-hour workweek are not available on a broad scale, though a number of smaller-scale experiments have been carried out in recent years.

EXAMPLES OF REDUCED-HOURS, FIVE-DAY WORKWEEKS

The French 35-hour workweek that was discussed in Chapter 2 produced positive feedback from workers, who were the main policy target of the Socialist Party government of Lionel Jospin that was elected in 1997. A total of 60% of workers surveyed said that their everyday lives had improved, while 13% said they had deteriorated (Lehndorff 2014). Estrade and Meda (2002) found that managers expressed greater satisfaction than unskilled laborers, while the numbers overall were as in Lehndorff (2014) – about 60% of people were more satisfied with the quality of their daily lives under the 35-hour workweek and 10–15% of people were less satisfied.

The productivity impacts were difficult to ascertain because the French policy was implemented unevenly in different companies and in the government sector, and it was implemented partially in 2000 and further in 2002, after which government policy changed when the Conservative Party gained power. Several studies did show marginal but positive improvements in worker productivity after the first phase of implementation. For example, Gubian et al. (2004) found that, up to the time of their study, hourly productivity gains, wage moderation, and the reduction of payroll tax allowed firms at 35 hours to maintain their competitiveness. Askenazy (2013) found that the impact on productivity was extremely nuanced, because not all firms participated in the 35-hour workweek and because work time flexibility was greatly increased for employers in many cases, thus countering the reduced number of hours, among other factors. On balance, he found that employee hourly productivity did indeed increase with the shorter workweek.

An experiment in Sweden in 2016 has allowed a handful of organizations to offer their employees a five-day, 30-hour workweek with six-hour days. The workers in the organizations involved are paid the same as they received for 40-hour workweeks. This arrangement has produced a very positive statement of satisfaction from employees and judgment by employers that the workers are more productive in the shorter workdays, so that no extra cost was incurred except for needing to hire additional employees to staff the organizations during the regular work hours (Alderman 2016).

MOTIVATION AND PRODUCTIVITY IN EXAMPLES OF FOUR-DAY, 32-HOUR WORKWEEKS

A number of US companies have moved to four-day, reduced-hours workweeks, with generally positive outcomes in terms of both motivation and productivity. For example, at 37Signals (renamed Basecamp in 2014), a small software company in the Midwest, the workweek has been cut to four days and 32 hours during the summer months from May to October. The CEO, Jason Fried, claims that the company has produced results during those months equal to the results during the winter months, when the traditional five-day, 40-hour schedule is followed. Unfortunately, no direct measurement was made to demonstrate the productivity levels across the year, so the example is just anecdotal.[8]

Treehouse, an online education company with 85 employees, has followed a four-day, 32-hour workweek for ten years. The company's CEO asserts that employee retention is excellent compared with similar tech firms and that employees are more productive when they have the extra day of personal time each week. He also claims that productivity has improved noticeably as people come in on Mondays very refreshed after the long weekend. As with the previous example, no precise measurement has been done to support the anecdotal observations.[9]

Google's 20% Rule, Lockheed's Skunk Works et al.

Another model that has been implemented at several tech companies is to allow employees to spend a percentage of their time working on projects of their own interest. This is reflected in the one-time Google policy of allowing employees to spend up to 20% of their time working on projects of their own choice, as long as the intent was to generate benefits for Google.[10] This policy was announced by the company in 2004, and then formally discontinued in 2014, apparently due to managers' difficulties in achieving their targets when employees were spending time on these other projects.

This idea is not new – examples include earlier efforts to entice employees to work on innovative, independent projects at Lockheed's Skunk Works[11] in California, which produced several major aircraft designs, including the U2, the SR71 Blackhawk, and the F-22 Raptor. This Lockheed program was initiated in 1943. The 3M program of allowing employees 15% of their time for independent projects, which was launched in 1948, led to the development of sandpaper, DVDs, and Post-it Notes,[12] among many other innovations.[13]

Not surprisingly, these employers and many others with similar innovation-oriented policies populate the list of Forbes Top 100 Employers in the United States.[14]

In a macro context, one can perhaps extrapolate from the course of the past century and project into the future that the net benefits of the four-day workweek will be positive for employee motivation and satisfaction, as they have been for previous workweek reductions since the late 1800s. Even so, the challenges of implementing the four-day, 32-hour workweek include the likelihood that the program will be initiated by a limited number of organizations (e.g., as with Ford Motor Company moving to the 40-hour workweek in 1926), so many workers will continue to face the existing workweek conditions, while those who are able to enter into the 32-hour workweek will probably be positive about their experience as much from the novelty as from the actual motivation involved.[15]

PRODUCTIVITY INCREASES IN THE US OVER THE YEARS

The overall level of US productivity (defined as output/man hour) has increased fairly consistently for more than a century. Table 3.1 describes the rate of increase of output/man hour over the past 140 years.

Alternatively, the Bureau of Labor Statistics (2018) has demonstrated the rate of US productivity growth since 1947 (see Figure 3.1). This figure shows somewhat of a rollercoaster ride of productivity increase over the years, with three periods of increasing productivity growth through the 20th century and the early 21st century and three periods of decreasing productivity growth, including in the past decade.

Table 3.1 Improvements in Living Standards, 1870–2010

Period	Total Factor Productivity (Average Annual Growth Rate)	Main Sources of Growth	Change in Life Expectancy at Birth (Years per Decade)
1870–1900	~1.5–2%	Transportation, communications, trade, business organization	1.3
1900–1920	~1%		3.2
1920s	~2%	Electricity, internal combustion engines, chemicals, telecommunications	5.6
1930s	~3%		3.2
1940s	~2.5%		5.3
1950–1973	~2%	Widespread	1.4
1973–1990	<1%		2.4
1990s	>1%	Information technology	1.7
2000s	~1.5%		1.4
1870–2010	~1.6–1.8%		2.3
1950–2010	~1.2–1.5%		1.8

Source: Shackleton (2013, p. 5).

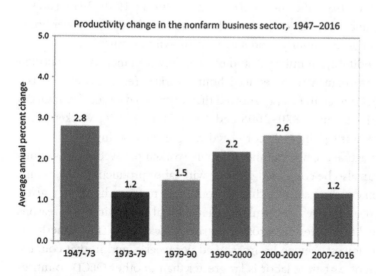

Figure 3.1 Productivity Growth in the United States, 1947–2016
Source: Bureau of Labor Statistics, www.bls.gov/lpc/prodybar.htm.

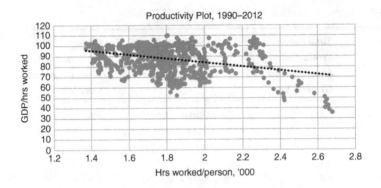

Figure 3.2 Hours Worked and Productivity in OECD Countries, 1990–2012

Source: OECD, https://data.oecd.org/lprdty/gdp-per-hour-worked.htm and https://stats.oecd.org/Index.aspx?DataSetCode=ANHRS. Figure constructed by the author.

Even with changes in the rate of technology development, productivity in the US has grown fairly steadily for almost one and a half centuries at about 1.5–2% per year. Gordon (2010), nevertheless, is somewhat pessimistic about the next two decades, forecasting productivity growth of just under 1.5% per year through to 2027.[16]

With respect to productivity across countries, there is quite a bit of evidence on the relationship between hours worked and worker output/hour. Data from the 34 OECD countries during 1990–2012 show a strong linear correlation between hours and productivity – fewer hours result in greater hourly productivity as shown in Figure 3.2.

In addition, a number of studies have shown an increase in reported job performance with reduced hours worked (e.g., Kossek and Lee 2008). Cette et al. (2011) showed that, over two data sets from OECD countries during 1870–2005 and 1950–2005, greater worker productivity was significantly correlated with fewer working hours.

The actual average number of hours worked per week across countries can also be compared globally with labor productivity. This comparison does not show a change from more to fewer hours in a given context, and it does ignore many other cultural and institutional reasons for the different results across countries. For example, The Netherlands has the lowest average hours worked per week – and in that country, the use of part-time labor is far greater than in other OECD countries (27% of men and 77% of women). So it is not clear that the average full-time Dutch workweek is actually that low in comparison with the

Motivation and Productivity

other countries, where full-time employment is the norm for most people. Even so, it is clear that the countries with the lowest average hours worked (see Table 2.1 presented in Chapter 2) are generally the ones that have highest labor productivity (OECD 2018).[17]

CONCLUSIONS

From the various studies of reduced workdays and hours per week in the 1970s and more recently, it does appear that worker satisfaction has risen with a lower number of hours worked per week or a lower number of days worked per week. It is also apparent from the evidence that worker satisfaction is highest at the time of implementing a shorter workweek, and then it tends to tail off somewhat over time. Still, the net result is consistently a higher level of satisfaction with fewer work hours and/or days per week.

It is clear from the evidence presented in this chapter that output per hour of work has increased over time in every study of reduced work hours that has been done around the world in the past 150 years. This does *not* say that overall output rose with fewer hours worked, but that hourly output per person rose and continues to rise through the years.

NOTES

1 This assumes, of course, that people who want to continue working for 40 hours or more per week will be able to do so. The 32-hour workweek just becomes the standard workweek, so that 40 hours would include eight hours of overtime work. Greater choice should produce greater satisfaction and motivation.

2 Although we did use some measures of happiness in Chapter 2 as indicators of satisfaction with work.

3 Silvestro speculated that this finding resulted from the fact that more satisfied workers generally worked in smaller supermarkets, while larger supermarkets tended to be more profitable.

4 Adding a bit of silliness to the findings, the authors discovered that the office coffee and doughnut concession reported a 32% increase in the average employee expenditure once the four-day workweek was implemented.

5 http://le.utah.gov/audit/10_10arpt.pdf.

6 In 8% of the companies, the four-day, 40-hour workweek was considered a failure and was dropped. See Wheeler et al. (1972, p. 5).

7 See, for example, State of Utah (2010). *A Performance Audit of the Working 4 Utah Initiative.* July. https://le.utah.gov/audit/10_10arpt.pdf.

8 See Stephanie Vozza (2015). "How These Companies Have Made Four-Day Workweeks Feasible", Fastcompany. June 17, www.fastcompany.com/3047329/the-future-of-work/how-companies-actually-make-four-day-workweeks-feasible.

9 See Andy Clark (2015). "America's Fantasy of a Four-Day Workweek", *The Atlantic*. June 23, www.theatlantic.com/business/archive/2015/06/four-day-workweek/396530/.

10 This program is described in a *New York Times* article: www.nytimes.com/2007/10/21/jobs/21pre.html.

11 See, for example, www.lockheedmartin.com/us/aeronautics/skunkworks.html.

12 See, for example, https://hbr.org/2013/08/the-innovation-mindset-in-acti-3.

13 A commentary on this 3M policy over several decades appears in Chapter 5 of Verne Harnish, The Greatest Business Decisions of All Time. Fortune, 2011, https://books.google.com/books?id=IuDqBQAAQBAJ&pg=PT41&lpg=PT41&dq=policy+of+allowing+employees+15%25+of+time+for+independent+projects&source=bl&ots=_A7ZVlxbBZ&sig=rUVg9HhVUR-urIKIzw0Uifx_JNU&hl=en&sa=X&ved=0ahUKEwiB56L45YPVAhUG4iYKHZucDv84ChDoAQghMAA#v=onepage&q=policy%20of%20allowing%20employees%2015%25%20of%20time%20for%20independent%20projects&f=false.

14 Forbes' 2017 list appears in www.forbes.com/best-employers/list/#tab:rank_search:google.

15 This phenomenon is often called the "Hawthorne effect" after the study showing that workers were more productive initially when a work rule change occurred because they knew they were being observed and they reacted positively to being observed rather than to the work rule.

16 Gordon (2010) estimated a longer range of growth in US multi-factor productivity (MFP), as shown here: Gordon (2010). Table 4: Output, Inputs, and MFP Growth, Non-Farm Non-Housing Private Economy, New and Old Data, 1891–2007

Years	Output	Labor	Capital	MFP
1891–1913	4.48	2.68	4.46	1.26
1913–1928	3.13	1.10	2.84	1.51
1928–1950	4.08	0.67	0.86	3.36
1950–1964	3.51	1.16	3.18	1.75
1964–1972	4.18	1.85	4.52	1.53
1972–1979	3.70	2.34	3.63	0.98
1979–1988	3.06	1.47	3.40	1.01
1988–1996	2.92	1.47	2.38	1.18
1996–2007	3.60	1.15	2.82	1.95

His longer-term results show productivity growth closer to 1.5% per year since 1891.

17 A Spearman rank correlation between the top 30 countries in productivity and those same countries measured for hours worked per week is −0.80 − a strong 80% negative correlation between productivity and hours worked.

REFERENCES

Alderman, L. (2016). "In Sweden, an Experiment Turns Shorter Workdays Into Bigger Gains", www.nytimes.com/2016/05/21/business/international/in-sweden-an-experiment-turns-shorter-workdays-into-bigger-gains.html?_r=0.

Askenazy, P. (2013). "Working time regulation in France from 1996 to 2012", *Cambridge Journal of Economics*. Vol. 37, 323–347.

Bird, R. (2010). "The Four-Day Work Week: Old Lessons, New Questions", *Connecticut Law Review*. Vol. 42, pp. 1059–1080.

Bureau of Labor Statistics (2018). "Labor Productivity and Costs". www.bls.gov/lpc/prodybar.htm.

Calvasina, E.J. and W.R. Boxx (1975). "Efficiency of Workers on the Four-Day Work Week", *Academy of Management Journal*. Vol. 18, pp. 604–610.

Cette, G., S. Chang, and M. Conte (2011). "The Decreasing Returns on Working Time: An Empirical Analysis on Panel Country Data", *Applied Economics Letters*. Vol. 18, pp. 1677–1682.

Estrade, M.-A. and D. Méda (2002). *Principaux Résultats de l'Enquête RTT et Modes de Vie*. Paris: Direction de l'Animation de la Recherche, des Études et des Statistiques. http://travail-emploi.gouv.fr/IMG/pdf/Les_principaux_resultats_de_l_enquete_RTT_et_Modes_de_vie.pdf.

Facer, R. and L. Wadsworth (2010). "Four-Day Work Weeks: Current Research and Practice", *Connecticut Law Review*. Vol. 42, pp. 1031–1046.

Goodale, J.G. and A.K. Aagaard (1975). "Factors Relating to Varying Reactions to the 4-Day Workweek", *Journal of Applied Psychology*. Vol. 60, pp. 33–38.

Gordon, R. (2010). "Revisiting U.S. Productivity Growth over the Past Century with a View of the Future", NBER Working Paper #15834. Cambridge, MA: NBER.

Grant, A. (2008). "Does Intrinsic Motivation Fuel the Prosocial Fire? Motivational Synergy in Predicting Persistence, Performance, and Productivity", *Journal of Applied Psychology*. Vol. 93, pp. 48–58.

Gubian, A., S. Jugnot, F. Lerais, and V. Passeron (2004). "Les Effets de la RTT sur l'Emploi: Des Simulations Ex Ante aux Évaluations Ex Post", *Économie et Statistique*. Vol. 376–377, pp. 25–54.

Harter, J., F. Schmidt, and T. Hayes (2002). "Business-Unit-Level Relationship Between Employee Satisfaction, Employee Engagement, and Business Outcomes: A Meta-Analysis", *Journal of Applied Psychology*. Vol. 87, pp. 268–279.

Hodge, B.J. and R.D. Tellier (1975). "Employee Reactions to the Four-Day Week", *California Management Review*. Vol. 18, pp. 25–30.

Ivancevich, J.M. (1974). "Effects of the Shorter Workweek on Selected Satisfactions and Performance Measures", *Journal of Applied Psychology*. Vol. 59, pp. 717–721.

Ivancevich, J.M. and H. Lyon (1977). "The Shortened Workweek: A Field Experiment", *Journal of Applied Psychology*. Vol. 62, pp. 34–37.

Kossek, E.E. and M.D. Lee (2008). "Implementing a Reduced-Workload Arrangement to Retain High Talent: A Case Study", *The Psychologist-Manager Journal*. Vol. 11, pp. 49–64.

Lehndorff, S. (2014). "It's a Long Way from Norms to Normality: The 35-Hour Week in France", *Industrial & Labor Relations Review*. Vol. 67, pp. 838–863.

Lyubomirsky, S., K.M. Sheldon, and D. Schkade (2005). "Pursuing Happiness: The Architecture of Sustainable Change", *Review of General Psychology*. Vol. 9, pp. 111–131.

Nord, W.R. and R. Costigan (1973). "Worker Adjustment to the Four-Day Week: A Longitudinal Study", *Journal of Applied Psychology*. Vol. 58, pp. 60–66.

Ng, S.T., R.M. Skitmore, K.C. Lam, and A.W.C. Poon (2004). "Demotivating Factors Influencing the Productivity of Civil Engineering Projects", *International Journal of Project Management*. Vol. 22, pp. 139–146.

OECD (2018). GDP per Hour Worked. https://data.oecd.org/lprdty/gdp-per-hour-worked.htm.

Poor, R. (1970). "Reporting a Revolution in Work and Leisure: 27 4-Day Firms", in *4 Days, 40 Hours*, ed. R. Poor. Cambridge, MA: Bursk & Poor, pp. 15–37.

Ronen, S. and S. Primps (1981). "The Compressed Work Week as Organizational Change: Behavioral and Attitudinal Outcomes", *Academy of Management Review*. Vol. 6, pp. 61–74.

Shackleton, R. (2013). "Total Factor Productivity Growth in Historical Perspective", US Congressional Budget Office Working Paper #2013-1. March, www.cbo.gov/sites/default/files/113th-congress-2013-2014/workingpaper/44002_TFP_Growth_03-18-2013_1.pdf.

Silvestro, R. (2002). "Dispelling the Modern Myth: Employee Satisfaction and Loyalty Drive Service Profitability", *International Journal of Operations & Production Management*. Vol. 22, pp. 30–49.

Steele, J.L. and R. Poor (1970). "Work and Leisure: The Reactions of People at 4-Day Firms", in *4 Days, 40 Hours*, ed. R. Poor. Cambridge, MA: Bursk & Poor, pp. 69–92.

Wheeler, K., R. Gurman, and D. Tarnowieski (1972). *The Four-Day Week: An AMA Research Report*. New York: American Management Association.

Four

For the first movers onto the four-day workweek, how will they use the additional eight hours of "free" time? There is no doubt that some people will choose to remain with 40 hours of work, and so they will either choose overtime at their main job or find another job to fill in eight more hours of work during the week. But what about everyone else?

One way to look at this question is to ask another: how do people divide up their time into various types of activity? Of course they have to sleep, and at least most people have to work to produce income to pay the bills. An early effort to investigate Americans' use of their time by Robinson and Godbey (1997) led them to categorize time use in four areas: Productive, Maintenance, Expressive, and then Travel involved in each of the areas. Figure 4.1 shows this organization of activities.

For each person in a household, it presumably will be necessary to work for income to pay for housing, food, clothing, health care, education, etc. So, the first category of "Productive Time" has a subcategory of "Contracted Time," which implies working for some organization – though self-employed people fit here as well. The second subcategory of work called "Committed Time" involves home-related activities such as childcare, shopping for household needs, cooking and cleaning, etc., which are presumably not compensated but are still necessary activities.

The second broad heading of time use is "Maintenance," meaning primarily sleeping to refresh the body, eating to sustain it, and grooming activities. Once again, these are necessary activities for a household, though the amounts of time assigned to them may vary somewhat from one person to another.

The final main category of activities is "Expressive," or what might just be called "Leisure" items, such as watching TV, involvement in

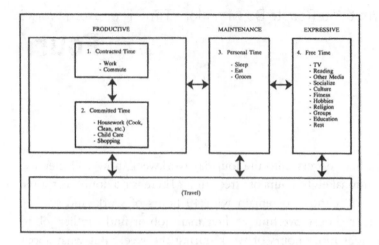

Figure 4.1 Four Kinds of Time Use
Source: Americans' Use of Time Project.

cultural/civic activities, exercising, studying, and many more. This is the area most affected by the four-day workweek, since additional time would be available for these activities beyond what is available today. "Travel" related to each of the three main activities is placed in a separate box, which is probably a useful idea, since one might view that as a necessary cost of pursuing the main activities and something that people could try to minimize through lifestyle adjustments.

While there is nothing fundamental about this division of time use into the four categories, this structure does point out quite usefully the decisions that people must make between more (or less) work and less (or more) leisure. The allocations to maintenance, committed time, and travel are much less flexible, though they do respond somewhat to choices in the first two areas.

When the workweek is reduced to four days, then people will have to choose among time allocations in the four areas of Figure 4.1. For those who continue to work for 40 hours per week, there would not be any necessary reallocation. For people who reduce the amount of time spent on "Contracted Time" working, they then will expand their time in the other areas. Since people tend to sleep more on weekends anyway, they probably will do so on the additional weekend day. Since they have more time to deal with "Committed Time" chores such as housework and shopping, they probably will expand these activities as well. And then they will have much more time still available for the "Expressive" or leisure activities, from watching more TV to becoming more involved in social and cultural activities. It is quite difficult to try to extrapolate time uses from current conditions to the situation when people work one day less per week, but there are some indicators discussed below that may help in anticipating those time reallocations.

With respect to business activity, given the trends in the amount and uses of leisure time during the past half-century, one would expect growth to occur in leisure-related activities and thus in businesses that provide leisure activities. These range from entertainment such as watching TV, movies, sports, and arts, to participation in sports and arts, to education. New jobs should be generated in these areas as more people choose to spend more time pursuing these activities. Figure 4.2 shows a US Government estimate of the percentage of time that people 15 years and older spend on various activities today.

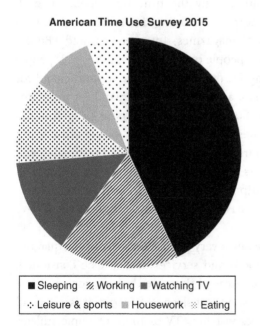

American Time Use Survey 2015

■ Sleeping ⁒ Working ■ Watching TV
∴ Leisure & sports ▩ Housework ⁖ Eating

Figure 4.2 Time Spent on Primary Activities by Americans in 2015
Source: US Bureau of Labor Statistics, 2016, www.bls.gov/tus/tables/a1_2015.pdf.

The chart shows that Americans on average used more than a third of their time for sleeping and only about a sixth for working, including getting to work, on an average day.[1] Leisure and sports accounted for another 20% of time use, most of which was for watching television, as shown in the first column of Table 4.3. No other single activity took up more than 5% of people's time, except if housework is combined with caring for children and others in the household, which together constituted about 10% of time for Americans in 2015.

Based on this survey of existing time use in the US, one might expect greater leisure time to require more supply of TV content, communications media, reading materials, and sports opportunities, among other things. Educational activity may be expected to increase as well, along with shopping trips and time spent caring for family members. Eating, drinking, and doing household chores constitute another three hours per day, and potentially also could increase.

The additional employment generated in these activities would be some percentage of the additional time available to people working only 32-hour weeks multiplied by the time they spend in each activity. If people spend more time reading, for example, then they will consume more books, magazines, Internet use, and eBooks, which in turn require more people producing those things. If people spend more time watching TV, then there will be more demand for TVs and other video devices, as well as more demand for programming for them to watch. Both more TVs and more programming will have to be produced, hence generating more jobs in those fields. And if people choose to pursue healthier lives, they presumably will spend more time in sports and recreational activities, which will boost the demand for equipment and places to pursue those activities such as parks and gymnasiums. More of these things will have to be produced as well.

It is not possible to generate a very precise estimate of the quantity of additional non-work goods and services that will be consumed, nor in which of the various areas of time use they may occur. While it is a safe bet that people won't just sleep 20% more, it is not at all clear if more couch potatoes watching TV or more Olympic athletes pursuing sports will result from the greater availability of time. Two possible sources of insight into the uses of time include surveys of

Table 4.1 Trends in American Time Use on an Average Workday

Activity/Hours per Day	1965	1975	1985	2005	2015
Sleeping	7.6	7.9	7.7	8.6	8.6
Working	4.4	4.0	4.0	3.7	3.5
Watching TV	1.5	2.2	2.2	2.6	2.6
Eating	1.1	1.2	1.2	1.2	1.1
Household work	2.4	2.1	2.1	2.3	2.2
Personal care	1.6	1.6	1.7	0.8	0.8
Entertainment	1.3	1.1	1.1	2.2*	1.8*
Shopping	0.9	0.8	0.9	0.8	0.7
Recreation	0.5	0.6	0.7	0.3	0.3

* Measured as leisure other than watching TV.

Sources: Data from Robinson and Godbey (1997) and US Bureau of Labor Statistics, American Time Use Surveys for 2005 and 2015.

people's time use since 1965, which demonstrate the trends that may be extended. Since those surveys are only (in the early years) for days of the workweek, it also would be useful to know what people do during weekends – which has been tracked now for more than a decade in newer US Department of Labor surveys.

Table 4.1 shows that people have been sleeping more in recent years than in the past. This change, however, is probably due to the slightly different methodologies used by Robinson and Godbey (1997) in the first three surveys during 1965–85 and the more recent ones used by the US Department of Labor since 2003. Regardless of this possible adjustment in the responses to make them more comparable, it appears that people are not sleeping less despite the presumed greater intensity of demands on their time in the 21st century.

Another perspective on potential shifts in time use can be noted using data collected by Steele and Poor (1970) relating to the four-day, 40-hour workweek that was implemented by some companies at that time. These authors found that the people who switched from a five-day workweek to a four-day workweek stated that they increased a variety of activities with the extra weekend day. The most cited, included in decreasing order, were: swimming and boating; working a second job; resting; buying a vacation home; and engaging in political action work.

An additional study done at that same time (Nash 1970) speculated that with the extra weekend day people would spend more on vacation housing and on recreation, part-time education, and religious contributions. Nash speculated that significant additional spending would take place on travel to vacation spots and on provision of food and housing for those vacation spots.

Work has been declining as a percentage of total time over the past 50 years to an average of 3.5 hours per day (including transport to and from work) in 2015. This number should be read with care, because it relates to all Americans over age 15, whether they are employed or unemployed, students, part-time employees, etc. If we look just at people who have full-time employment, as shown in the third column of Table 4.3, it is clear that these people are working just about eight hours per day during the workweek. So, the reason for the decline in hours worked per week in the past half-century has to do with more people working part-time and more people being either outside of the workforce or categorized elsewhere (e.g., as students).[2]

A separate perspective that is useful here to explore the expected allocation of time during an additional weekend day is to look just at time use during weekends, as shown in Table 4.2.

So, if people have one more weekend day available each week, they will presumably, according to their habits since 2005, use that day to spend more time sleeping and watching TV – but also much

Table 4.2 Time Use during Weekends, 2005 and 2015

Activity/Hours per Weekend Day	2005	2015
Sleeping	9.3	9.4
Working	1.3	1.3
Watching TV	3.1	3.3
Eating	1.4	1.3
Household work	2.6	2.6
Personal care	0.8	0.8
Entertainment	3.0*	2.8*
Shopping	0.9	0.9
Recreation	0.3	0.4

* Measured as leisure other than watching TV.

Source: Data from US Department of Labor, BLS, www.bls.gov/news.release/pdf/atus.pdf.

less time working and a bit more time in entertainment and in household work as compared to their weekday behavior. This can be seen by comparing Table 4.2 with the last two columns of Table 4.1. Unfortunately, we cannot go back earlier than 2003 with these data, since such information was not collected in earlier efforts. Even with more hours of sleep and watching TV, it appears that people are likely to have another 11 hours or so during the new weekend day for other activities.

Given the trends in non-work activity over the past 50 years, it really is not clear what activities will be favored when the four-day workweek opens up another day for people's choices, other than probably more sleep and more TV watching on the added weekend day. Still, to generalize in order to focus on the additional hours, we can make a simple claim that perhaps half of the additional time that people enjoy away from work in the four-day workweek will be used for additional consumption of goods and services that must newly be produced for housework, leisure, and personal care activities. This implies an increase in employment in those sectors of about 10% on top of existing employment on the new weekend day,[3] everything else equal.[4] So the impact on jobs would be enormous, given that for the one day it would constitute 10%/7 days per week = 1.4% of employment today, which would be about 2 million people in the US. That would push unemployment down by 25%, since there were just under 8 million unemployed people in June 2016.[5] While it would take time for the full impact of the 32-hour, four-day workweek to be realized as more companies switch to the new structure, the eventual boost to employment in the sectors producing "weekend consumption" goods and services could be substantial.[6]

The preferences revealed by people in the US time use studies include one potential bias that is not quantifiable. The choice of quantities of time spent in leisure and in studies, among others, depends on the person initially holding a job that generated income sufficient to pursue those additional activities. So, there must be a hidden preference for work to "pay the bills," such that a decline in work hours due to loss of a job would produce drastic changes in the other activities. This preference is not explicit because the person in the surveys already does hold a job or is in a situation (e.g., a dependent child over 15 years old) that enables him/her to pursue the current activities.

Repeating a point made earlier in this book: this discussion should not be confused with the logic of a four-day workweek in which people work ten hours per day to accomplish a 40-hour workweek in four days. That model has been fairly widely discussed (e.g., see, for example, Hellriegel 1972; Ronen and Primps 1981; Peeples 2009; Bird 2010, and Chapter 3 above). That model focuses on the ideas that job satisfaction may increase when more days are free for non-work activities; commuting costs are reduced when people only commute four days per week; and facility usage costs are reduced when all employees have three-day weekends.[7] While these are benefits of placing more daily work into fewer days, the idea in the present situation is to actually reduce the number of hours worked. So a four-day week would have 32 hours of work, not 40.

SECTORS THAT WOULD FACE INCREASED DEMAND

Looking at the set of activities that are pursued more during weekends than weekdays, we can perhaps disaggregate a bit more than above. Table 4.3 shows more details of people's 2015 allocations of time among various activities on an average weekday versus an average weekend day.

Based on the information in Table 4.3, we can see that people spend much more time during weekend days sleeping and watching TV. They also spend more time in lawn and garden care, in home maintenance, and in religious and volunteer activities. People also spend more time socializing and participating in sports. Those with children spend more time with them during the weekend days. And of course they spend much less time working, though the average is still about 1.2 hours of work per weekend day for everyone, and 5.6 hours per weekend day for those who work on those days.

The impact of this additional weekend activity will be to generate greater demand for the products and services needed for lawn and garden care, home maintenance, social activities, and sports, among others. Whether this translates into a 10% increase in demand for such products and services or less (or more) than that, the result will still be an increase in demand for them. This is very much like Henry Ford's

Table 4.3 Time Spent in Detailed Primary Activities, Averages per Day on Weekdays, 2015 Annual Averages

Activity	Average Hours per Day, Civilian Population		Average Hours per Day for Persons Who Engaged in the Activity	
	Weekdays	Weekends and Holidays	Weekdays	Weekends and Holidays
Total, all activities	24.00	24.00	n/a	n/a
Personal care activities	9.42	10.17	9.42	10.18
Sleeping	8.59	9.40	8.60	9.42
Grooming	0.70	0.66	0.84	0.87
Health-related self-care	0.10	0.08	1.38	1.41
Personal activities	0.01	0.01	1.29	1.48
Travel related to personal care	0.01	0.02	0.45	0.76
Eating and drinking	1.12	1.33	1.17	1.41
Eating and drinking	1.03	1.17	1.08	1.24
Travel related to eating and drinking	0.09	0.16	0.43	0.58
Household activities	1.71	2.16	2.24	2.80
Housework	0.52	0.71	1.48	1.77
Food preparation and cleanup	0.59	0.62	1.01	1.18
Lawn and garden care	0.17	0.25	1.88	2.25
Household management	0.12	0.15	0.68	0.84
Interior maintenance, repair, and decoration	0.06	0.08	2.36	2.33
Exterior maintenance, repair, and decoration	0.05	0.10	1.73	2.30
Animals and pets	0.11	0.12	0.60	0.78
Vehicles	0.03	0.05	1.61	1.44
Appliances, tools, and toys	0.02	0.02	0.99	1.48
Travel related to household activities	0.04	0.06	0.42	0.57
Purchasing goods and services	0.70	0.85	1.62	1.86
Consumer goods purchases	0.31	0.50	0.79	1.12
Grocery shopping	0.09	0.13	0.70	0.83

[continued]

Table 4.3 [Cont.]

Activity	Average Hours per Day, Civilian Population		Average Hours per Day for Persons Who Engaged in the Activity	
	Weekdays	Weekends and Holidays	Weekdays	Weekends and Holidays
Professional and personal care services	0.10	0.04	1.07	1.00
Financial services and banking	0.01	[1]	0.28	0.24
Medical and care services	0.07	0.01	1.38	2.07
Personal care services	0.02	0.01	1.25	1.24
Household services	0.02	0.01	0.76	0.63
Home maintenance, repair, decoration, and construction (not done by self)	0.01	[1]	1.06	1.45
Vehicle maintenance and repair services (not done by self)	0.01	[1]	0.78	0.59
Government services	[1]	[1]	0.74	[2]
Travel related to purchasing goods and services	0.27	0.31	0.66	0.70
Caring for and helping household members	0.54	0.45	2.04	2.11
Caring for and helping household children	0.41	0.37	1.84	2.13
Caring for and helping household adults	0.04	0.03	0.65	0.57
Travel related to caring for and helping household members	0.10	0.05	0.61	0.63
Caring for and helping non-household members	0.17	0.23	1.63	1.74
Working and work-related activities	4.47	1.28	8.42	5.80
Working	4.04	1.17	7.93	5.55
Work-related activities	0.01	[1]	[2]	[2]
Other income-generating activities	0.03	0.02	3.14	2.09
Job search and interviewing	0.04	0.01	2.44	1.89
Travel related to work	0.35	0.09	0.78	0.68
Educational activities	0.58	0.19	6.36	3.53

Activity				
Attending class	0.34	0.02	4.99	3.67
Homework and research	0.18	0.15	2.92	3.20
Travel related to education	0.04	0.01	0.68	0.74
Organizational, civic, and religious activities	0.24	0.55	1.88	2.76
Religious and spiritual activities	0.08	0.32	1.09	1.96
Volunteering (organizational and civic activities)	0.14	0.16	2.12	2.49
Travel related to organizational, civic, and religious activities	0.02	0.07	0.45	0.47
Leisure and sports	4.69	6.43	4.91	6.62
Socializing, relaxing, and leisure	4.22	5.76	4.45	5.96
Socializing and communicating	0.51	1.07	1.44	2.43
Relaxing and leisure	3.65	4.54	4.01	4.97
Watching TV	2.56	3.29	3.23	4.07
Arts and entertainment (other than sports)	0.05	0.15	2.75	2.72
Sports, exercise, and recreation	0.30	0.38	1.39	1.92
Participating in sports, exercise, and recreation	0.29	0.35	1.36	1.85
Attending sporting or recreational events	0.01	0.03	2.37	2.66
Travel related to leisure and sports	0.18	0.29	0.57	0.70
Telephone calls, mail, and e-mail	0.16	0.16	0.71	0.88
Telephone calls (to or from)	0.10	0.12	0.70	0.89
Household and personal messages	0.06	0.04	0.50	0.56
Travel related to telephone calls	[1]	[1]	0.38	0.29
Other activities, not elsewhere classified	0.20	0.19	1.35	1.55

1 Estimate is approximately zero.

2 Estimate is suppressed because it does not meet the American Time Use Survey publication standards.

n/a: Not applicable.

Note: A primary activity refers to an individual's main activity. Other activities done simultaneously are not included.

Data refer to persons 15 years of age and over.

Source: American Time Use Survey, Bureau of Labor Statistics.

idea that if people have more time and money available to them, they will buy more consumer goods, including his cars.[8]

SPENDING PATTERNS IN THE 20TH CENTURY

If we go back a little further in time, it was estimated that during the 20th century, the greatest expenditures from consumers' incomes went on food and housing. Then, after World War II, there were major advances in medicine (penicillin, better surgical techniques, and greater company spending on worker health plans). These led to much greater spending on health care, which has continued into the 21st century (Lebergott 1993).

Table 4.4 shows major spending categories for people in the US from 1900 to 1990.

Perhaps not surprisingly, food, clothing and housing expenses (house ownership or rental plus household expenses such as electricity, water, furniture, appliances, etc.) tended to parallel the increases in overall consumer spending during the 20th century in the US. What grew most as a proportion of total spending were medical expenses – no surprise to those living in the early 21st century! Transportation also became a much larger percentage of total consumer spending over the century, as did recreation. Table A4.2 in Appendix 4.1 below provides data from 2012 to 2014 on consumer spending patterns, using a somewhat different set of categories, but demonstrating the large allocations to housing, transportation, and health care.

These data do not show directly the changes in people's preferences for working versus other activities, though the increase in recreation clearly implies an increase in time used for that purpose. The increase in health care spending may indicate greater time (and money) spent on consumption of that service, although rising health care costs may constitute the bulk of that increase.

CONCLUSIONS

When given the opportunity to have a third weekend day, people will choose a variety of allocations of their additional available time. One choice undoubtedly will be for some people to use the eight hours that were previously worked to continue to work, for the same

Table 4.4 Personal Consumption, per Capita, by Major Group, USA (US dollars)

Spending Category/ Year	Total Spending	Food	Clothing	Housing	Household Operation	Transport	Recreation	Education	Health Care
1900	3,266	1,416	272	256	465	141	83	38	171
1910	3,891	1,670	442	310	495	13	121	45	210
1920	3,667	1,121	410	353	486	88	184	53	240
1930	4,227	1,207	390	421	576	385	220	63	275
1940	4,491	1,479	385	437	629	446	224	63	273
1950	5,741	1,713	446	652	794	751	291	81	431
1960	6,698	1,866	440	930	890	816	297	116	618
1970	8,842	2,102	525	1,313	1,166	1,070	445	203	1,018
1980	10,746	2,141	690	1,754	1,384	1,207	655	227	1,522
1990	13,051	2,193	920	1,898	1,626	1,621	1,026	298	1,928

Source: Data taken from Lebergott (1993, Appendix A).

employer or another one. As the idea of the 32-hour, four-day work-week becomes more established, more and more people will reallocate those eight hours of newly available time to leisure, housework, education, and other uses.

As a result, more products and services of these types (viz. leisure, housework, and education) will need to be produced. This will stimulate additional output in these sectors of the economy. While we cannot be sure of the allocation of this time and the consumption of these products and services, it is reasonable to expect that they will expand in a similar proportion to the total time use that they occupy today. So, we would expect important expansions of personal care (particularly sleeping), educational activities, and watching TV, along with other non-work activities.

APPENDIX

Use of time on an average day

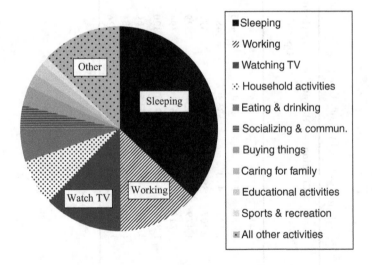

Figure A4.1 Use of Time on an Average Day

The chart shows that Americans on average used a third of their time for sleeping and less than 20% for working – since the average is calculated across a seven-day week for all people including students, part-time workers, and unemployed people and most people do not work during the two weekend days.

Source: US Bureau of Labor Statistics, 2014, www.bls.gov/news.release/pdf/atus.pdf.

Table A4.1 Detailed List of Activities of Employed People, 2015

	Average Hours per Day for Persons Who Engaged in the Activity		
	Total	Men	Women
Personal care activities	9.65	9.44	9.85
Sleeping	8.84	8.78	8.90
Grooming	0.85	0.72	0.96
Health-related self-care	1.39	1.16	1.53
Personal activities	1.34	1.55	0.91
Travel related to personal care	0.54	0.56	0.52
Eating and drinking	1.24	1.30	1.19
Eating and drinking	1.12	1.17	1.08
Travel related to eating and drinking	0.48	0.49	0.47
Household activities	2.41	2.13	2.61
Housework	1.58	1.23	1.71
Food preparation and cleanup	1.05	0.82	1.19
Lawn and garden care	2.00	2.30	1.57
Household management	0.72	0.68	0.75
Interior maintenance, repair, and decoration	2.35	2.51	2.09
Exterior maintenance, repair, and decoration	1.96	2.29	1.36
Animals and pets	0.65	0.68	0.63
Vehicles	1.54	1.70	0.91
Appliances, tools, and toys	1.13	1.34	0.70
Travel related to household activities	0.47	0.54	0.41
Purchasing goods and services	1.70	1.50	1.86
Consumer goods purchases	0.90	0.77	0.99
Grocery shopping	0.74	0.72	0.76
Professional and personal care services	1.06	0.91	1.13
Financial services and banking	0.27	0.27	0.27
Medical and care services	1.42	1.53	1.37
Personal care services	1.24	0.58	1.42
Household services	0.73	0.63	0.81
Home maintenance, repair, decoration, and construction (not done by self)	1.10	0.83	1.25
Vehicle maintenance and repair services (not done by self)	0.74	0.68	0.81
Government services	0.71	0.73	0.70
Travel related to purchasing goods and services	0.67	0.65	0.69
Caring for and helping household members	2.06	1.61	2.32
Caring for and helping household children	1.91	1.46	2.16
Caring for and helping household adults	0.63	0.64	0.62

(continued)

Table A4.1 (Cont.)

	Average Hours per Day for Persons Who Engaged in the Activity		
	Total	Men	Women
Travel related to caring for and helping household members	0.62	0.57	0.64
Caring for and helping non-household members	1.66	1.68	1.65
Working and work-related activities	8.03	8.40	7.58
Working	7.57	7.89	7.19
Work-related activities	1	0.99	1
Other income-generating activities	2.89	1.93	3.38
Job searching and interviewing	2.40	2.79	1.70
Travel related to work	0.77	0.84	0.68
Educational activities	5.79	6.26	5.39
Attending class	4.94	5.13	4.76
Homework and research	2.99	3.08	2.92
Travel related to education	0.69	0.70	0.68
Organizational, civic, and religious activities	2.23	2.28	2.20
Religious and spiritual activities	1.52	1.54	1.50
Volunteering (organizational and civic activities)	2.23	2.21	2.25
Travel related to organizational, civic, and religious activities	0.46	0.48	0.45
Leisure and sports	5.42	5.77	5.09
Socializing, relaxing, and leisure	4.91	5.16	4.67
Socializing and communicating	1.78	1.77	1.80
Relaxing and leisure	4.30	4.58	4.02
Watching TV	3.48	3.70	3.26
Arts and entertainment (other than sports)	2.73	2.68	2.77
Sports, exercise, and recreation	1.54	1.75	1.29
Participating in sports, exercise, and recreation	1.49	1.71	1.24
Attending sporting or recreational events	2.51	2.34	2.75
Travel related to leisure and sports	0.62	0.63	0.61
Telephone calls, mail, and e-mail	0.75	0.71	0.78
Telephone calls (to or from)	0.76	0.76	0.76
Household and personal messages	0.51	0.50	0.52
Travel related to telephone calls	0.36	0.38	0.34
Other activities, not elsewhere classified	1.40	1.54	1.30

1 Estimate is suppressed because it does not meet the American Time Use Survey publication standards.

Note: A primary activity refers to an individual's main activity.

Other activities done simultaneously are not included. Data refer to persons 15 years of age and over.

Source: American Time Use Survey, Bureau of Labor Statistics.

Table A4.2 Average Annual Expenditures and Incomes (US$) of All Consumer Units and Percentage Changes for Selected Components, 2012–14

Item	2012	2013	2014	Percentage Change	
				2012–13	2013–14
Average income before taxes	65,596	63,784	66,877	−2.8	4.8
Average annual expenditures	51,442	51,100	53,495	−0.7	4.7
Food	6,599	6,602	6,759	0	2.4
Food at home	3,921	3,977	3,971	1.4	−0.2
Food away from home	2,678	2,625	2,787	−2.0	6.2
Housing	16,887	17,148	17,798	1.5	3.8
Shelter	9,891	10,080	10,491	1.9	4.1
Owned dwellings	6,056	6,108	6,149	0.9	0.7
Rented dwellings	3,186	3,324	3,631	4.3	9.2
Apparel and services	1,736	1,604	1,786	−7.6	11.3
Transportation	8,998	9,004	9,073	0.1	0.8
Gasoline and motor oil	2,756	2,611	2,468	−5.3	−5.5
Vehicle insurance	1,018	1,013	1,112	−0.5	9.8
Health care	3,556	3,631	4,290	2.1	n/a
Health insurance	2,061	2,229	2,868	8.2	n/a
Entertainment	2,605	2,482	2,728	−4.7	9.9
Cash contributions	1,913	1,834	1,788	−4.1	−2.5
Personal insurance and pensions	5,591	5,528	5,726	−1.1	3.6
All other expenditures	3,557	3,267	3,548	−8.2	8.6

n/a: Because of the questionnaire change for health insurance, the 2013–14 percentage change is not strictly comparable to prior years.

Source: US Department of Labor, 2015, www.bls.gov/news.release/pdf/cesan.pdf.

NOTES

1 This is confusing because that main table includes all seven days of the week and also includes unemployed people, students, and a few other complicating features. So it appears that work represents only about half the hours we normally discuss. If we focus on just those who are in full-time employment, as in Table 4.3, we see that they spend about eight hours of a typical workday at work and just 1.5 hours working during weekend days.

2 Unemployment could be another factor in the work time reduction over the years, but the rate of unemployment has not moved permanently up or down from about 5% overall. Unemployment was far above 5% during the Global Financial Crisis and today is below 5%. It was also well above that level after the oil price shocks in the 1970s and below 5% for most of the period after World War II and before 1971. See, for example, http://data.bls.gov/timeseries/LNU04000000?years_option=all_years&periods_option=specific_periods&periods=Annual+Data.

3 The 10% value is equal to half of the eight additional hours per week not used for work. Those four hours are 10% of the 40-hour workweek. This value could also

be seen as one more day of non-work (24 hours) minus eight hours of sleep = 16 additional hours during which to consume more. From this, 16 hours/168 hours per week = about 10% of the week.

4 Everything else is not equal, since under our assumption everyone will start with a 10% pay cut and thus will be able to purchase 10% fewer goods and services. This will dampen the increased spending significantly, but not completely.

5 See www.bls.gov/news.release/empsit.nr0.htm.

6 This estimate is not at all precise and it could be inaccurate due to fewer people taking up the four-day workweek, more switching of people's purchases away from traditional items to leisure items (rather than just increased purchasing in the leisure area), and many other factors. The logic for the four-day workweek is not dependent on the generation of new jobs, even though that is possible, as suggested.

7 Interestingly, Allen and Hawes (1979) found that people were significantly more positive about a four-day, 40hour workweek if they had plans to use the additional time for more non-work activities.

8 Although not discussed earlier, in 1914, Ford Motor Company had literally doubled the wages of its factory workers. This produced a major increase in productivity as well as a big jump in consumer spending by the employees affected. See, for example, www.saturdayeveningpost.com/2014/01/03/history/post-perspective/ford-doubles-minimum-wage.html and www.npr.org/2014/01/27/267145552/the-middle-class-took-off-100-years-ago-thanks-to-henry-ford.

REFERENCES

Allen, R. and D. Hawes (1979). "Attitudes toward Work, Leisure, and the Four Day Workweek", Human Resources Management. Vol. 18, pp. 5–10.

Bird, R. (2010). "The Four-Day Work Week: Old Lessons, New Questions", Connecticut Law Review. Vol. 42, pp. 1059–1080.

Bureau of Labor Statistics (various years). American Time Use Survey. Washington, DC: US Department of Labor, www.bls.gov/tus/.

Hellriegel, D. (1972). "The Four-Day Work Week: A Review and Assessment", MSU Business Topics, Vol. 20, pp. 39–48.

Lebergott, S. (1993). Pursuing Happiness. Princeton, NJ: Princeton University Press.

Nash, W. (1970). "Implications for Urban America", in 4 Days, 40 Hours, ed. R. Poor. Cambridge, MA: Bursk & Poor, pp. 182–193.

Peeples, L. (2009). "Should Thursday Be the New Friday? The Environmental and Economic Pluses of the 4-Day Workweek", Scientific American, July 24. www.scientificamerican.com/article/four-day-workweek-energy-environment-economics-utah/.

Robinson, J. and G. Godbey (1997). Time for Life: The Surprising Ways Americans Use their Time. State College, PA: Penn State University Press.

Ronen, S. and S. Primps (1981). "The Compressed Work Week as Organizational Change: Behavioral and Attitudinal Outcomes", Academy of Management Review. Vol. 6, pp. 61–74.

Steele, J.L. and R. Poor (1970). "Work and Leisure: The Reactions of People at 4-Day Firms", in 4 Days, 40 Hours, ed. R. Poor. Cambridge, MA: Bursk & Poor, pp. 69–92.

Five

INTRODUCTION

The compensation issue is a major challenge. If people work 20% fewer hours, they should receive 20% less pay, other things equal. Some people may feel that this is an acceptable price to pay in exchange for greater free time to pursue other activities (such as raising children, pursuing education, or just leisure). Most people probably would see this as an overwhelming psychological and economic burden to accept. Alternatively, if companies were to allow a move to the 32-hour week without reducing weekly wages, then workers would be happy but the companies would face an enormous burden – unless hourly productivity increased so much as to offset the fewer hours worked. So, the challenge is to identify a process through which the goal of a four-day week is achieved without overly burdening either individuals or companies.

Let us begin this consideration by recognizing that hourly workers are the easiest to identify and measure for the reduction in work hours. For a doctor or attorney or educator, the reduced hours would only come from the fact that one more day of the week would be part of the weekend, and thus not subject to normal workplace activity. Even so, these professional workers would probably end up working fewer hours when their clients would switch to the four-day workweek and people in general would view Fridays as part of the regular three-day weekend.

SIX SCENARIOS

It is probably easiest to visualize the impact on compensation and costs to companies if we specify a number of possible ways in which the four-day workweek could be implemented in financial terms. In other words: who will pay for the reduction in hours and (partial) reduction in output caused by the move from five eight-hour days to four eight-hour days each workweek?

A few scenarios of how to achieve the four-day workweek follow. First, we assume that the workers will absorb the cost of reduced hours and reduced wages. Second, we assume that the workers and the companies share in the cost of reduced work hours and presumably somewhat reduced output. And finally, we assume that companies will bear the entire burden and consider how this might play out.

Scenario 1

The clear first step is for a company or group of companies to unilaterally declare the four-day, 32-hour workweek as the norm. Workers who chose to maintain their hours would have to work eight overtime hours per week, and this would maintain their wages at the original level. The workers who accept the 20% lower worktime and 20% lower wages would be the pioneers in this new world of work. In this first scenario, companies would not adjust their hourly pay rates and so they would have to hire additional workers to fill in the lost time – but at no greater cost.[1] We would see how people choose to use their time in this new environment, in which some percentage of workers would simply accept the new 32-hour workweek along with lower income and others would continue at 40 hours per workweek without losing income.

The result of this step would likely be that, over a few years, an increasing number of people would choose the shorter workweek as the pioneers demonstrate the benefits (and costs) involved. It is not likely that productivity would stand still, and companies may find that they could increase wages to some extent due to the higher hourly productivity of people working 32-hour weeks. In any event, after a few years with this model of work in operation, it is likely that people will accept the new four-day norm and view the workweek from that perspective. At some point, the federal government will probably mandate the 32-hour workweek as the standard for government offices and possibly some industries or types of employers – such as companies involved in inter-state commerce – just as happened 12 years after Ford Motor Company's launch of the 40-hour, five-day workweek in 1926.

Scenario 2

A second possibility for moving to the four-day, 32-hour workweek would be to spread the pain over time in order to allow the lower

Compensation

incomes and work outputs to be realized in increments. For example, everyone who moves to the 32-hour workweek could receive a 10% pay cut (instead of 20%), and then they could be offered the option of working overtime to recoup that lost income if they wish. A 2% additional annual pay cut would then continue for five more years, being potentially offset if productivity increased enough to enable the cuts to be eliminated sooner, so that companies could be approximately compensated for the overall 20% reduction in work time from employees.[2] This second arrangement would produce a 10% reduction in earnings for workers who move to the 32-hour workweek and a 10% higher initial cost of production for companies – unless productivity improved to reduce or eliminate this cost burden. If the companies adjusted their wage payments downward in subsequent years by enough to eliminate the cost/output gap over three or four years, then they would be back to the original trajectory of cost/unit of output after the adjustment period. Meanwhile, workers would only have suffered a 10% wage cut for a 20% work time reduction in year 1.

This gets messy because it just is not clear how much hourly productivity will improve when people have the shorter workweek. The previous scenario sketched out how companies and workers would be affected assuming no productivity increase, but that assumption is highly unlikely. This second scenario does not necessarily imply a productivity increase, but if one does occur, it could be as large as 10%, which would completely offset the 10% wage difference for companies. The workers would still suffer 10% reduced incomes for the first year in exchange for 20% fewer hours worked, before resuming their wage trajectory over time. Since we cannot be sure just how much more output will be generated per hour in the shorter workweek, the assertion of expected costs and benefits must remain a bit uncertain.

Scenario 3

Since we considered one alternative in which the workers incurred all of the costs of reduced work hours – and consequent reduced wages – let's consider a third scenario in which the companies incur all of the costs. If companies maintain weekly wage levels for their workers who move to the 32-hour workweek, then the companies will suffer a 20%

increase in their production costs, *ceteris paribus*. Of course, the companies would be anticipating an increase in productivity that would eliminate part or all of this cost, but unless the full productivity gain of 20% occurred in year 1, then companies and other employers would simply face higher costs and lower profits. If this were to occur, some companies would probably go out of business and the consequences overall would be pretty severe. In short, no sensible company would agree to this step unless either the government subsidized it somehow and/or if increased productivity were expected.[3] A government subsidy is easily imaginable – corporate taxes could be cut by some percentage for those firms that institute the four-day workweek while not cutting worker compensation.

Scenario 4

A fourth alternative could be for companies to anticipate the higher hourly productivity (as Henry Ford correctly did in 1926) and expect that wages would not have to be dropped by 20% to maintain output quantities achieved under the existing 40-hour workweek. Although we cannot estimate precisely how much added hourly output would be generated to partially or fully replace the lost eight hours per week of work, we could make some assumptions. If we assume that there will be a 10% increase in hourly productivity as a result of the reduced workweek, then companies could cut wages by only 10% and thus retain output and costs at their current levels by hiring new workers to fill in the four hours per week needed for each existing worker who moves to the four-day workweek. Existing workers would now have to accept a 10% cut in wages (or work four hours per week of overtime to keep their wages the same). This would clearly be more acceptable to workers than a 20% wage cut, but it is still a negative consequence of switching to the shorter workweek.

This fourth scenario is probably the closest one to what will actually happen when the four-day workweek is launched. Productivity is highly likely to rise, as it has in previous instances of workweek reductions. There is no reason to think that increased productivity will exactly offset the 20% reduction in hours worked, so some imbalance will likely occur. Thus, we will be left with some adjustment cost to be borne by someone. The easiest, most manageable way to carry out the reduction of one workday per week would probably be to cut 10% of wages to workers, leaving companies to absorb the higher costs implied and allowing workers to pick up the four hours of over-time that would leave their earnings unchanged, if they so choose (Scenario 5 in Table 5.1). Companies would have 10% higher wage costs minus the amount of greater production due to the expected increase in productivity. Within a couple of years, it is likely that the burden will have been eliminated by productivity improvements.

These five scenarios are summarized in Table 5.1, which shows a total of six possible outcomes depending on whether productivity increases or not and whether wages are reduced or not.

The sixth scenario in Table 5.1 is presented just for completeness. It shows the outcomes if wages were not cut and companies incurred the whole added cost, except that higher productivity helps out to partially close the gap. In this case, workers would be happy, since their wages would not be reduced; only 12.5% more workers would be needed to maintain output; and the companies would face a 10% higher cost of producing that output.

Table 5.1 Impacts of a Four-Day Workweek on Workers and Employers

Scenario/ Impact	Productivity	Impact on Workers	Impact on Companies	Other Impacts
20% wage cut; Scenario 1	No change	Large income loss	No loss, no gain[4]	25% added workers needed[5]
10% wage cut; Scenario 2	No change	10% income loss	10% higher cost	12.5% added workers needed
No wage cut; Scenario 3	No change	No loss	20% output loss[6]	Implies costs up
20% wage cut; Scenario 4	10% higher	10% income loss*	No loss, no gain	12.5% added workers needed
10% wage cut; Scenario 5	10% higher	No income loss*	10% output loss or higher cost	12.5% added workers needed
No wage cut; Scenario 6	10% higher	10% higher income*	10% output loss or higher cost	12.5% added workers needed

These scenarios assume that workers move from a 40-hour workweek to a 32-hour workweek, thus reducing their worktime by 20% (four days instead of five).

* Assuming that workers are compensated 10% for the extra 10% productivity.

WORKER RESPONSES AND POSSIBLE GOVERNMENT POLICIES

Repeating a point already made: for anyone who feels the need to maintain his/her income path under the new 32-hour workweek (which implies a 20% pay reduction), the option is available to do so, and if we assume that overtime up to total work of 40 hours per week is paid at the same rate as regular income, then the cost to companies would not go up for those people. That is, everyone who wants to continue working 40-hour weeks can do so, with the last eight hours considered as "overtime." And if the pay cut is just 10%, because we might assume that there will be a 10% productivity increase, then these workers would only have to work four more hours (36 hours total per week) to maintain their existing incomes.

If the government wanted to support the shift to a four-day work-week, then it could offer tax benefits to companies in exchange for implementing the shorter workweek. Under all of the scenarios except the two where workers incur all of the costs (Scenarios 1 and 4), an arrangement could be made for companies to receive tax credits or deductions related to the wages of workers who move to the four-day workweek. The tax benefits could be structured to just offset the higher costs to companies of allowing workers to work 32 hours per week instead of 40, or these benefits could be less, leaving some of the burden on companies. This also assumes that companies will choose to maintain their levels of output, hiring new workers to fill in the time needed to get back to that level after existing workers reduce their hours by 20%.

Even for the two scenarios where workers bear all of the costs, a government policy could be implemented to lower the personal income taxes of those people who choose the four-day workweek. Thus, as with the case of a corporate tax subsidy, the government would bear the cost of the transition until labor productivity recouped the lost hours and output returned to its previous rhythm of increase over time. An interesting quirk of this arrangement is that workers would have to be responding to their after-tax incomes rather than their gross incomes. If they are tax-blind, then the tax break would not stimulate the workers to accept the 32-hour workweek.

The critical element is to maintain the three-day weekend so that work is not just shifted around in a contractual sense. This arrangement of allowing workers to choose how many hours to work in the range of 32–40 hours per week would provide fewer additional jobs than forcing everyone to take the 32-hour workweek, since unquestionably some people would choose to work overtime rather than dropping to the lower number of hours and lower pay (except in Scenarios 3 and 6, where pay is not reduced). Even so, people likely would choose to reduce their hours in the future if the psychological framing of the workweek says that 32 hours is "normal."[7]

Companies of course would not be enthusiastic about reducing worker compensation by 10% and losing worker hours by 20% (Scenario 2) at the initial point of launching this new shorter workweek – unless productivity immediately jumps by 10% as assumed in Scenario 5. Even if productivity (output per hour) caught up with the lower number of hours over a five-year horizon, there still would be a loss for the companies, particularly in the first year. The numbers could be adjusted to find some happy medium point, but fundamentally the cost of the initial reduction in hours will either have to be borne by the companies, the workers, or some combination of them, as sketched above. For those hourly workers who choose to remain at 40 hours of work per week, there would be no adjustment cost. The underlying issue here is productivity. If workers turn out to be more productive per hour with the shorter workweek, this could justify the smaller downward wage adjustment that is being proposed for those who move to 32 hours of work per week.[8]

AN EMPIRICAL CHECK ON PRODUCTIVITY VS. HOURS WORKED AND WAGES

Productivity gains, wages, and work hours over the past several decades in the US are shown in Figure 5.1. It is clear that productivity tracks wages, with gains always remaining slightly or greatly above wage increases. And it is also evident that the workweek has basically not changed at all during that 25-year time period of 1988–2013. It is very encouraging for our argument to see that productivity has grown at about 2–4% per year during the period and that wages have grown at 1–2% per year. With any productivity boost at all from the shorter workweek, companies will be able to absorb the fewer hours worked fairly quickly. A number of studies have shown that a reduction in working hours consistently leads to increased productivity per hour – though not necessarily enough to keep total output the same.[9]

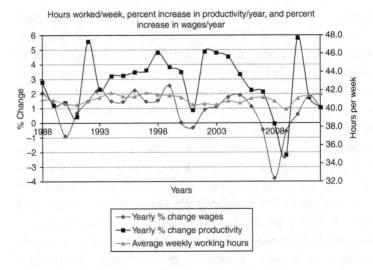

Figure 5.1 US Workweek, Δ Productivity and Δ Wages over Time

Sources: http://elibrary-data.imf.org/DataExplorer.aspx; www.bls.gov/lpc/#tables; https://research.stlouisfed.org/fred2/series/AWHMAN/.

While it may appear that productivity growth has fluctuated wildly since the 2008 financial crisis, it still does appear to be positive and above the rate of wage increases even during the most recent half-decade (except for 2009). And if we consider a longer time period such as the 25 years shown in Figure 5.1, or 50 or 100 years in the US, it is clear that productivity increases have exceeded wage increases overall and fairly consistently.[10]

A part of the compensation issue should include the time opened up for other activities during the week for those people who choose to move to the 32-hour workweek. That is, they will now have one extra day of "free" time to pursue other activities – including, if they choose, to moonlight at another job and earn more income. The argument of this book is that people will choose some combination of activities to fill the extra eight hours available per week. It does not matter what their choices are; they still will be better off by having the choice.[11]

A CONSIDERATION OF US INCOME INEQUALITY

Despite the rise in productivity since 1980, the incomes of the bottom 20% of the US income distribution have not risen in real terms over these past three and a half decades. Income inequality is a major

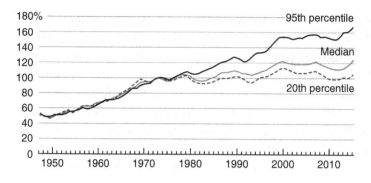

Figure 5.2 Income Gains Widely Shared in Early Postwar Decades – But Not Since Then

Note: In 2014, Census split its sample of survey respondents into two groups to test a set of redesigned income questions. In 2015 (reporting on 2014 incomes using the new questions), Census released two estimates of 2013 incomes, one based on the old questions and one on the new. The chart uses the estimate based on the old questions, based on Center on Budget and Policy Priorities' judgment that, due in part to sample size, it is likely to be more accurate for 2013.

Source: Center on Budget and Policy Priorities calculations based on US Census Bureau Data; Center on Budget and Policy Priorities (2016, p. 9).

concern for governments and for society at large.[12] It has become especially visible since the Global Financial Crisis in the form of the Occupy Wall Street[13] protest in 2011 and subsequent criticism of the top 1% of wealth holders by the "other 99%." While this opposition to the enormous disparity in incomes and wealth between that top 1% and everyone else has not coalesced around a policy direction, one can see an obvious pressure toward taxing the rich more significantly and redistributing income more widely.

Figure 5.2 shows the growth in income inequality in the US since the 1970s. The results in Figure 5.2 are striking: the top 5% of American families had an increase in their average real incomes of about 70% since 1980, while the bottom 20% had essentially no real income increase and the median family enjoyed just a 20% increase over 35 years. Among other things, this implies that the productivity gains shown in Figure 5.1 have not been significantly shared by most employees and have been received largely by people at the very top end of the income and wealth distributions.

Given this situation today, it appears that some greater degree of income redistribution may be in store for the US in the future. Whether this is accomplished by higher taxation of people at the top end of the income distribution, higher minimum wages for people at the bottom of the income distribution, or some combination of these or other policies is not at all clear. In any event, it does not just automatically follow that increases in hourly productivity will lead to parallel increases in labor compensation, so our assertions that wages can be raised in step with productivity require some effort to be realized.

CONCLUSIONS

The challenge of distributing the costs of a reduced-hours workweek across companies and employees is not a simple one. It depends very much on the improvements in hourly productivity that arise from the shorter workweek. If employees work 20% fewer hours each week (e.g., taking off Fridays), will outputs at their companies drop by 20%? Or will they drop by somewhat less than that as the employees become more productive in the hours that they do work? Or will production magically remain unchanged as productivity gains exactly offset hours reductions? Obviously, this last possibly exists but is not likely. So, how should the burden of shifting to this new workweek be shared?

Various scenarios are presented above, showing what the costs might be and who would bear them. A key element of the plan is that anyone wishing to remain working enough to maintain his/her income (the same number of hours as before or somewhat fewer due to productivity increases) will be allowed to do so. There will be some complications in carrying out this policy, since some jobs are not divisible such that the person could work an extra four to eight hours per week if the company is closed on Fridays. Despite the likelihood of such adjustment costs, the four-day workweek is feasible and the distribution of costs and benefits is manageable. The government could support the shift to the 32-hour workweek by offering temporary tax deductions to companies that implement it and/or tax reduction plans for employees who agree to move to the shorter workweek and take a reduced income as a result. This government policy would place some of the burden on all taxpayers, probably ensuring a backlash – but also ensuring that the whole society helps to pay for the transition.

NOTES

1 It is unlikely that wages would remain constant, since hiring new people would presumably require a higher wage rate to attract them.

2 This is a sleight of hand, because the 10% pay cut, if productivity does not rise by at least that amount, will mean that companies (i.e., employers) will have to incur the initial loss of the other 10% of output. If this loss is recouped over a few subsequent years, as suggested in the text, then the employers will be back to even after the adjustment period. Make no mistake, however; there is a non-trivial adjustment cost involved unless productivity really jumps.

3 For example, when the French government imposed the 35-hour workweek in 2000, they offered tax breaks to companies for complying with this policy. See, for example, Askenazy (2013).

4 Assuming that companies can hire additional workers to replace lost output at the same wages.

5 As pointed out in Chapter 1, 25% more workers will be needed to replace the 20% reduction in hours of existing workers, since the new workers also will work just 32 hours per week. So eight hours per week of lost working time is a quarter of a new employee's time. Similarly, a loss of 10% of existing workers' hours would require 12.5% of a new worker's time at the new standard of 32 hours of work per week.

6 Companies either accept lower output or higher costs to maintain existing output.

7 The behavioral economics concept of "framing" is extremely important here. If people come to believe that "normal" is a four-day, 32-hour workweek, then they will put their overall activities into this structure and look at the rest of their time as available for leisure, a second job, or some other use. See, for example, Tversky and Kahneman (1986).

8 Workers who choose to drop to 32 hours per week could be given the full 20% pay cut, and in this way companies would not face any added burden except to recruit more people to fill in the work hours needed. This solution would initially dissuade more people from choosing the 32 hour workweek, but it would produce the same results over time as people come to accept the new norm.

9 An International Labour Office study (Golden 2012) cites numerous analyses in which reduced work hours produced greatly increased productivity in manufacturing and in services in the US and other OECD countries; see www.ilo.org/wcmsp5/groups/public/---ed_protect/---protrav/---travail/documents/publication/wcms_187307.pdf.

10 See Bureau of Labor Statistics data from earlier years (e.g., www.bls.gov/lpc/prodybar.htm).

11 As noted previously, a person could choose to work the extra eight hours at his/her existing job and earn the same income as before. If this were the case, then that person would be no better off and no worse off. So, the situation is "Pareto optimal" because it leaves many people better off and some people no worse off.

12 See, for example, Piketty et al. (2016).

13 This movement is described in its webpage, http://occupywallst.org/. Discussion of the movement appears in www.washingtonpost.com/national/on-leadership/ what-is-occupy-wall-street-the-history-of-leaderless-movements/2011/10/10/ gIQAwkFjaL_story.html and in www.theatlantic.com/politics/archive/2015/06/ the-triumph-of-occupy-wall-street/395408/.

REFERENCES

Askenazy, P. (2013). "Working time regulation in France from 1996 to 2012", *Cambridge Journal of Economics.* Vol. 37, pp. 323–347.

Center on Budget and Policy Priorities (2016). *A Guide to Statistics on Historical Trends in Income Inequality.* Washington, DC: Center on Budget and Policy Priorities, www.cbpp.org/research/poverty-and-inequality/a-guide-to-statistics-on-historical-trends-in-income-inequality.

Congressional Research Service (2016). *The U.S. Income Distribution: Trends and Issues.* Washington, DC: CRS, https://fas.org/sgp/crs/misc/R44705.pdf.

Golden, L. (2012). *The Effects of Working Time on Productivity and Firm Performance: A Research Synthesis Paper.* Geneva: International Labour Office, www.ilo.org/wcmsp5/groups/ public/---ed_protect/---protrav/---travail/documents/publication/wcms_ 187307.pdf.

Piketty, T., E. Saez, and G. Zucman (2016). "Distributional National Accounts: Methods and Estimates for the United States", NBER Working Paper 22945, https://eml. berkeley.edu/~saez/Piketty-Saez-ZucmanNBER16.pdf.

Tversky, A. and D. Kahneman (1986). "Rational Choice and the Framing of Decisions", *Journal of Business.* Vol. 59, pp. S251–S278.

Six

INTRODUCTION

The thesis of this book is that the time has come for a four-day, 32-hour workweek. This is due to the production capabilities that exist in the world today and the logic that people should think about their use of time among work and other activities, especially since the workweek has been fixed at five days and 40 hours for almost a century. The argument is not that jobs are becoming fewer due to automation or any other factor. Nevertheless, it is instructive to review the recurring argument that has resurfaced over hundreds of years, namely that technology will replace humans and that insufficient jobs will remain for everyone who needs one.

The discussion below provides some historical background on the subject of automation versus unemployment (tracked for the US since World War II in Appendix A6.1), starting with the 19th century and moving up to today's context. The concern has not changed over 200 years, and the lessons are that: (1) people have not simply been replaced by machines, but new jobs have been created; and (2) we probably have not paid adequate attention to the people who are displaced by machines and the need to support them to get back into productive employment.

SOME HISTORY FROM THE 19TH AND 20TH CENTURIES

During the early 19th century, a group of workers in England calling themselves Luddites destroyed textile weaving machinery, since they argued that it was eliminating jobs rather than improving social well-being. In fact, the new textile manufacturing machines and the new manner of work were eliminating the jobs of weavers and other skilled clothing workers, who rejected this change.[1] This was not an isolated protest, but rather a major labor revolt involving large-scale property damage and several deaths during 1811–17. The movement was broadly stopped by intervention from the British Army and by the national government imposing harsh penalties on the Luddite leaders.[2] Nevertheless, the Luddite movement was a strong statement that people affected negatively by technology change will respond with opposition to it, sometimes to the point of violence. And in the aftermath of this revolt, during the early 1800s, employment in British clothing manufacture grew substantially, as companies built factories for mass producing clothes and employed hundreds or thousands of people rather than just a family in a "cottage" industry.[3]

An importance difference between 19th century mechanization and its late 20th century counterpart is that the earlier phenomenon was characterized by replacement of skilled workers by machines (e.g., skilled weavers by machine looms, and even skilled auto craftsmen with the assembly line), while the more recent process has eliminated more unskilled labor positions. Henry Ford's auto plants replaced, more or less, one skilled craftsman with 29 relatively unskilled assembly line workers.[4] In contrast, the mechanization of office work in the past 50 years has greatly reduced the number of secretaries and clerical staff – relatively low skilled – while increasing the number of computers as well as more skilled technical staff.

Concern about automation replacing humans and causing joblessness has never ceased since the Luddite times.[5] In an extensive review of the evidence on this subject during the 1800s and 1900s in the US, Gregory Woirol (1996) documented magazine and academic journal articles as well as pronouncements by US Government officials that recognized the simultaneous problems of greater automation and growing unemployment at various times. These articles typically coincided with periods of greater unemployment in the US and reflected the search for culprits to explain the problem. During periods of job growth and boom times in general, this argument was muted or almost non-existent.

Woirol (1996, p. 19) reasoned that there were four arguments as to why automation could create unemployment:

> (a) there may be a lack of markets for the increased output; (b) there may be a lack of capital to employ released labor; (c) the rise in purchasing power from technological change hypothesized by Say's Law compensation theory would not occur; and (d) technological change led to a constantly decreasing ratio of circulating to fixed capital.

These arguments were used by classical economists in the 1800s as well as by journalists and policy-makers through the years to question the greater use of machines to replace people in industry.

In the late 1920s, arguments appeared in the literature about how productivity had grown dramatically since World War I, while jobs in manufacturing were declining. This perspective arose from the Bureau of Labor Statistics' first publication of productivity data in 1922 and further publications in subsequent years. It was clear that during job downturns productivity was still growing. (What was missed, of course, is that during job upturns productivity was rising as well!)

A debate on the jobs/automation theme arose in the late 1920s, before the Depression. The US Secretary of Labor, James Davis, stated in 1927 that there was a danger of lack of employment due to the rapid adoption of new techniques of production. The *Journal of Commerce* in 1928 noted:

This country has upon its hands a problem of chronic unemployment, likely to grow worse rather than better ... Business prosperity, far from curing it, may tend to aggravate it by stimulating invention and encouraging all sorts of industrial rationalization schemes.

This is striking since the debate occurred during the 'Roaring 20s' and predated the Great Depression, though the arguments certainly continued and intensified during that following decade.[6]

Another wave of concern regarding "technological unemployment" occurred in the US during the early 1960s (Akst 2013). It led President Johnson to convene a blue-ribbon panel on the subject and the resulting publication of *Technology and the American Economy* (National Commission on Technology, Automation, and Economic Progress 1966). The Commission concluded broadly that technology was not leading to higher unemployment (which at the time was below 4%). Nevertheless, the Commission explicitly recognized that technology could harm people in particular jobs, and it recommended a range of government policies to assist those harmed by the overall beneficial technological changes. These policies included: public sector hiring, using the government as employer of last resort; a minimum wage; compensatory education for those in disadvantaged areas; and the creation of a national database to try to match job seekers with jobs. At about the same time as this Commission was working, the Vietnam War led to a large growth in military-related spending and hiring, such that unemployment remained below 4% for the rest of that decade and the jobs versus technology scare faded away.

A more likely era for concern about technological unemployment was the period of 1975–85, when the unemployment rate stayed stubbornly above 7% for most of the time, and reached almost 11% in 1982.[7] Despite this historically high level of unemployment, economists and journalists did not flock to the issue of automation as a key driver of the problem. They focused instead on the Organization of the Petroleum Exporting Countries (OPEC)-related oil crisis and the extremely high interest rates that were implemented to rein in inflation. (The Eurodollar deposit interest rate reached almost 21% in December 1980, and the US prime rate did likewise and then stayed above 20% for most of 1981.) The unemployment rate stayed relatively high compared to the historical average of about 5% until the late 1990s.

THE 21ST CENTURY

Mechanization of production has progressed to a point today in the 21st century where once again people question whether jobs can survive the onslaught of machines. Historically, this has been a false argument or concern, since employment has risen over time despite the increase in the use of machines. This has happened in the long run since the beginning of the industrial revolution in the 1700s, as well as in the short term, say, during the period of personal computers since 1980, or even during the life of the Internet since the mid-1990s. There are more jobs now than there were 20 years ago (Internet age) or 35 years ago (PC age) or since the dawn of the industrial age in about 1760. And this is true across countries, except recently in Japan, as shown in Table 6.1. Japan's slow GDP growth since the early 1990s and its negative population growth have both contributed to this decline in Japanese employment.

The employment situation in the US during the 21st century has been much more of a concern in light of the Global Financial Crisis than in relation to automation. With the dramatic increase in unemployment to over 10% of the US workforce in 2010, there was doubt about ever returning to a "normal" rate of 5% or less. This concern was fueled

Table 6.1 Number of Employed, in Thousands

Year	USA[1]	Germany[2]	UK[2]	Japan[3]
1920	27,340		9,768 (December 1922)	27,261
1930	29,409		10,535	29,600
1940	47,520		16,332	34,200
1947	57,038		15,351	36,200
1955	62,170	16,510[4]	21,671	40,896
1970	78,678	26,695[4]	22,909	50,939
1975	85,845	26,334[4]	25,056	52,230
1980	99,303	27,495[4]	25,327	55,360
1995	124,900	37,885	27,660	64,570
2007	146,047	37,989	29,118	64,120
2010	139,064	38,738	29,125	62,570
2014	146,305	39,879	30,642	63,506
2015	148,834	40,452	31,587	63,156
2016	151,436	40,552	31,907	63,042

1 USA: Bureau of Labor Statistics, www.bls.gov/cps/cpsaat01.pdf.

2 Germany, Japan, and UK: International Labor Organization, www.ilo.org/ilostat/faces/
help_home/data_by_country/country-details/indicator-details?country=GBR&subject=EMP
&indicator=EMP_TEMP_SEX_AGE_NB&datasetCode=YI&collectionCode=YI&_afrLoop=1293
235133886371#%40%3Findicator%3DEMP_TEMP_SEX_AGE_NB%26subject%3DEMP%26_
afrLoop%3D1293235133886371%26datasetCode%3DYI%26collectionCode%3DYI%26count
ry%3DGBR%26_adf.ctrl-state%3Dbxlvrhzv4_525.

3 Japan additional data from David Flath, *The Japanese Economy*, p. 52, https://books.google.ae/
books?id=_2DwAgAAQBAJ&pg=PA52&lpg=PA52&dq=japan+employment+1930&source=
bl&ots=tTpErD_BaG&sig=Eairlb59aTXHkLhz7JVOIPNXC3o&hl=en&sa=X&ved=0ahUKEwia_
sjN-MvKAhXBtBQKHQECDWQQ6AEIRjAK#v=onepage&q=japan%20employment%20
1930&f=false.

4 Employment during 1949–91 only includes West Germany (Federal Republic of
Germany).

Germany, the UK, and Japan, 2015 and 2016 data, www.ilo.org/ilostat/
faces/oracle/webcenter/portalapp/pagehierarchy/Page3.jspx?MBI_ID=32&_
afrLoop=1774548494226372&_afrWindowMode=0&_afrWindowId=rqy8q2qw3_
3501#!%40%40%3F_afrWindowId%3Drqy8q2qw3_3501%26_afrLoop%3D1774548494226
372%26MBI_ID%3D32%26_afrWindowMode%3D0%26_adf.ctrl-state%3Drqy8q2qw3_3533.

more by questions about government policies toward the financial
sector and competitiveness of US business rather than by machines
replacing people, but the automation issue remained there in the
background. Even so, the man vs. machine cloud reappeared by 2013
or 2014, as concerns about the Global Financial Crisis diminished and
as unemployment dropped down to below 7%. By the end of 2016,

with unemployment once again below 5%, much of the pressure was off. What remained was concern about jobs in particular sectors, particularly in manufacturing (as demonstrated by the Trump campaign and election), though even here the focus was on competition from foreign workers rather than on technology.

EMPLOYMENT AND AUTOMATION ACROSS INDUSTRY SECTORS

An important aspect of the job picture is the evolution of employment from agriculture to manufacturing to services. Looking back at US employment in 1900, approximately 41% of people worked in agriculture. This percentage dropped to less than 10% by 1950 and less than 2% by 2000. In 1950, about 34% of people worked in manufacturing; and by 2014 this percentage had dropped to 9%. And finally, in 1950, 59% of people worked in services, while by 2014 this percentage had grown to 84%.[8] Figure 6.1 shows these trends.

The number of jobs in the two traditional sectors certainly declined over these decades, but job growth in services greatly exceeded the losses in agriculture and manufacturing, as shown implicitly in Table 6.1. In more concrete terms, service sector employment went from just over 52 million jobs in 1970 to over 113 million jobs in

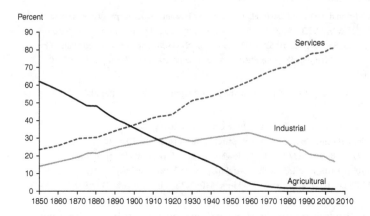

Figure 6.1 Distribution of US Employment by Sector, 1850–2008

Sources: International Historical Statistics (2013). "Market Services Productivity Across Europe and the U.S.," by Inklaar, R., M.P. Timmer, and B. van Ark, *Economic Policy*, Vol. 23, pp. 139–194; authors' calculations; http://static6.businessinsider.com/image/542dcc9669bedd6e532c06ec-1200-924/dallas%20fed%20us%20historical%20sectoral%20composition.png.

2010.[9] Clearly, services dominate the 21st-century job landscape. The question now is how the services sector jobs will evolve in the future.

While not a direct answer to the question, Table 6.2 disaggregates services activities into subsectors. During the 2004–14 period, health care, leisure and hospitality, and professional and business services were among the top five service sectors in employment and in terms of growth rates. Each of these three subsectors was larger by itself than total manufacturing employment during this time period, and each was growing faster than overall services and much faster than the overall economy.

Even with the optimistic history of job growth over time, the concern for job loss is very real today. Just as with the advent of outsourcing production of cars to Mexican assembly plants, iPhone assembly to China, and call centers to India, there is a real question about what will replace those jobs lost in the US and other Triad countries (mainly Japan, Canada, and Western Europe).[10] Digitalization and other machine use to replace human work continue to take away traditional jobs while adding new ones. There is certainly not a one-for-one replacement of old jobs with new jobs when mechanization occurs, so society has to find alternative employment for many of those who are replaced. The new jobs tend to be in services, which is good, because services already account for two-thirds or more of the economy in most countries today – 88% of the US economy – and employment opportunities are growing faster there than in manufacturing or mining/agriculture.

A problem with this kind of job substitution is that jobs in manufacturing are not necessarily replaced with equal-quality jobs in services. (The classic exaggeration is that the services jobs are mostly for hamburger flippers at McDonald's.) Of course, if the displaced employees move into computer programming or some other technology-intensive service, then the jobs may actually be more desirable and even better paid than those lost in manufacturing. Taking a look at the US Bureau of Labor Statistics list of top 10 jobs with the fastest growth rate in 2014 (Table 6.3) shows that they are all in services and that their average salaries are far above the average for all jobs. This certainly bodes well for the move from manufacturing into services for many people who find themselves looking for work – or for those who want to anticipate opportunities in the future.

It is important to note that the mechanization process affects not only manufacturing, but also services and primary industries such as

Table 6.2 US Employment by Major Industry Sector

Industry Sector	Thousands of Jobs			Change		Percentage Distribution			Compound Annual Rate of Change	
	2004	2014	2024	2004–14	2014–14	2004	2014	2024	2004–14	2014–24
Total	144,047.0	150,539.9	160,328.8	6,492.9	9,788.9	100	100	100	0.4	0.6
Non-agriculture wage and salary	132,462.2	139,811.5	149,131.6	7,349.3	9,320.1	92	92.9	93.0	0.5	0.6
Goods producing, excluding agriculture	21,815.3	19,170.5	19,227.0	-2,644.8	56.5	15.1	12.7	12.0	-1.3	0
Mining	523.2	843.8	924.0	320.6	80.2	0.4	0.6	0.6	4.9	0.9
Construction	6,976.2	6,138.4	6,928.8	-837.8	790.4	4.8	4.1	4.3	-1.3	1.2
Manufacturing	14,315.9	12,188.3	11,374.2	-2,127.6	-814.1	9.9	8.1	7.1	-1.6	-0.7
Services providing	110,646.9	120,641.0	129,904.6	9,994.1	9,263.6	76.8	80.1	81.0	0.9	0.7
Utilities	563.8	553.0	505.1	-10.8	-47.9	0.4	0.4	0.3	-0.2	-0.9
Wholesale trade	5,663.0	5,826.0	6,151.4	163.0	325.4	3.9	3.9	3.8	0.3	0.5
Retail trade	15,058.2	15,364.5	16,129.1	306.3	764.6	10.5	10.2	10.1	0.2	0.5
Transportation and warehousing	4,248.6	4,640.3	4,776.9	391.7	136.6	2.9	3.1	3.0	0.9	0.3
Information	3,118.3	2,739.7	2,712.6	-378.6	-27.1	2.2	1.8	1.7	-1.3	-0.1
Financial activities	8,105.1	7,979.5	8,486.7	-125.6	507.2	5.6	5.3	5.3	-0.2	0.6
Professional and business services	16,394.9	19,096.2	20,985.5	2,701.3	1,889.3	11.4	12.7	13.1	1.5	0.9

Educational services; private	2,762.5	3,417.4	3,756.1	654.9	338.7	1.9	2.3	2.3	2.2	0.9
Health care and social assistance	14,429.8	18,057.4	21,852.2	3,627.6	3,794.8	10.0	12.0	13.6	2.3	1.9
Leisure and hospitality	12,493.1	14,710.0	15,651.2	2,216.9	941.2	8.7	9.8	9.8	1.6	0.6
Other services	6,188.3	6,394.0	6,662.0	205.7	268.0	4.3	4.2	4.2	0.3	0.4
Federal government	2,730.0	2,729.0	2,345.6	–1.0	–383.4	1.9	1.8	1.5	0	–1.5
State and local government	18,891.3	19,134.0	19,890.1	242.7	756.1	13.1	12.7	12.4	0.1	0.4
Agriculture, forestry, fishing, and hunting	2,111.3	2,138.3	2,027.7	26.9	–110.5	1.5	1.4	1.3	0.1	–0.5
Agricultural wage and salary	1,149.0	1,384.0	1,307.3	235.0	–76.7	0.8	0.9	0.8	1.9	–0.6
Agricultural self-employed workers	962.3	754.3	720.4	–208.1	–33.8	0.7	0.5	0.4	–2.4	–0.5
Nonagricultural self-employed workers	9,473.6	8,590.2	9,169.5	–883.4	579.3	6.6	5.7	5.7	–1.0	0.7

Source: US Department of Labor, www.bls.gov/emp/ep_table_201.htm.

Table 6.3 Employment by Major Occupational Group, 2014 and Projected 2024 (Numbers in Thousands)

2014 National Employment Matrix Title	Employment		Change, 2014–24		Median Annual Wage (US$), 2016[1]
	2014	2024	Number	Percentage	
Total, all occupations	150,539.9	160,328.8	9,788.9	6.5	37,040
Management occupations	9,157.5	9,662.9	505.4	5.5	100,790
Business and financial operations occupations	7,565.3	8,197.8	632.4	8.4	66,530
Computer and mathematical occupations	4,068.3	4,599.7	531.4	13.1	82,830
Architecture and engineering occupations	2,532.7	2,599.9	67.2	2.7	77,900
Life, physical, and social science occupations	1,310.4	1,408.0	97.6	7.4	63,340
Community and social service occupations	2,465.7	2,723.4	257.7	10.5	42,990
Legal occupations	1,268.2	1,332.8	64.6	5.1	79,650
Education, training, and library occupations	9,216.1	9,913.7	697.6	7.6	48,000
Arts, design, entertainment, sports, and media occupations	2,624.2	2,731.7	107.5	4.1	47,190
Health care practitioners and technical occupations	8,236.5	9,584.6	1,348.1	16.4	63,420

1 Data are from the Occupational Employment Statistics program, US Bureau of Labor Statistics.

Source: Employment Projections program, US Bureau of Labor Statistics, www.bls.gov/news.release/ecopro.t04.htm.

mining and agriculture. So, most people would be moving from one service activity to another due to the increased mechanization of work. At the end of the day, there certainly is a risk of reduced employment opportunities due to mechanization, even if it has not been a problem historically. As shown in Table 6.2, employment opportunities at present appear to be greatest in health care, leisure and hospitality, and professional and business services. Judging from the continuing growth in jobs in these service sectors, the risk that "this time is different" appears to be limited, and there is room for optimism.

Other writers have explored the question of mechanization in some depth. Autor (2015a, p. 5) notes that "journalists and even expert commentators tend to overstate the extent of machine substitution for human labor and ignore the strong complementarities between automation and labor that increase productivity, raise earnings, and augment demand for labor." He goes on to say that in recent decades the kinds of tasks that have been complementary to automation include two broad categories, with the first being

> tasks that require problem-solving capabilities, intuition, creativity, and persuasion. These tasks, which we term "abstract," are characteristic of professional, technical, and managerial occupations ... [The] second broad category includes tasks requiring situational adaptability, visual and language recognition, and in-person interactions – which we call "manual" tasks. Manual tasks are characteristic of food preparation and serving jobs, cleaning and janitorial work, grounds cleaning and maintenance, in-person health assistance by home health aides, and numerous jobs in security and protective services.
>
> (Autor 2015a, p.12)

Overall, Autor is optimistic about the continuing demand for labor despite increasing mechanization of production.

As an example of how jobs are evolving in response to mechanization, a study by Bessen (2015) looks at the banking sector. He points out that despite the huge proliferation of automatic teller machines (ATMs) since 1980, the number of jobs for bank tellers has actually risen during 1980–2010. The tellers today tend to offer more services than just deposit-taking and cash disbursement; they are more like relationship bankers, offering help to clients with funds transfers, account management, credit cards, financial advice, etc.

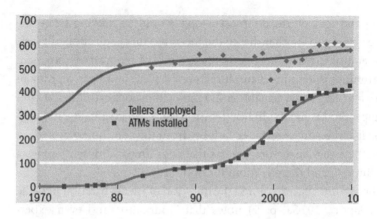

Figure 6.2 Dispensing Jobs

Source: Bessen, J. (2015). "Toil and Technology", *Finance & Development*, Vol. 52, p. 17.

This demonstrates the feature noted by Autor (2015b) that the new banking jobs require some abstract thinking and also situational awareness of the specific needs of each customer/client.

Approaching the recent trends in jobs and automation, Frey and Osbourne (2013) look at the likelihood of computerization of 702 job categories that existed in 2010 in the US. They find that, different from Autor and others who see the hollowing out of jobs toward lower-skilled and higher-skilled ones, computerization is expected to reduce the need for lower-skilled jobs in general. So, if their modeling turns out to be a good reflection of technological reality, the 21st century will show a migration of jobs to higher-skill, higher-wage categories that require social skills and creativity. According to their analysis, "most workers in transportation and logistics occupations, together with the bulk of office and administrative support workers, and labor in production occupations, are at risk" (Frey and Osbourne 2013, p. 44).

Goos et al. (2014) looked at the trajectory of jobs in 16 European countries during 1993–2010. They find, parallel to Autor et al. (2006), that technology was replacing jobs in the middle categories of skills, while high-skill and most low-skill categories of employment showed increases during this period. They also explore the impact of off-shoring of some economic activities as an alternative explanation for job displacement in the middle-skill category, finding that offshoring had less of an impact on the job trends than did technology development. The job categories that demonstrated the greatest growth and wage increases included the highest-paying managerial, professional, and associate professional occupations, followed by employees in services related to travel, catering, and personal care, and some low-paid elementary occupations including cleaners, domestic helpers, doorkeepers, porters, security personnel, and garbage collectors. The categories of jobs that suffered declines in Europe during this period included office clerks, craft and related trades workers, and plant and machine operators and assemblers – jobs that pay around the median occupational wage and generally require a medium level of skill.

Each of these empirical investigations found that overall job growth had occurred during the period in question (generally, the period since 1970 or so), while certain categories of employment suffered decreased wages and decreased job opportunities.

Looking forward to job growth in the US in the future, Alec Ross (2016) considers the impacts of robots and advances in biotechnology as they will affect the labor market. While his writing is more about the mindset that people need to have in the 21st century, his emphasis on the growing use of robots to perform more and more functions that have previously been done by humans is fully consistent with the other lessons presented in this chapter: namely, that people will have to learn skills that differentiate them from repeat-motion robots that are stronger and more effective at such tasks than human beings are. So, the direction of preparing for a job either in a business where skill is the key or where human interaction is key is a sensible path for future employment.

According to Ross (2016), the impact of biotechnology on the labor market is less clear, except that it implies greater opportunities for people who develop skills in this field. Biotechnology certainly will extend people's lifespans, and so preparing for jobs that relate to elderly people and to retired people is also a sensible path for job seekers to pursue today. This reality also implies that people in the age range of 65–80 or so may need to reconsider their retirement plans and aim to work for more years, since they are expected to live much longer than their predecessors.

McAfee and Brynjolfsson (2017) paint a very futuristic picture of employment in the years ahead. They argue that artificial intelligence is taking us to a point where production can be highly distributed, from 3D printing to design work done by robots, and that employment will have to shift to alternative activities and forms. Their interest is more in looking at how production is moving toward even greater mechanization through the use of artificial intelligence, but the implications are clear for employers and employees. They argue that decentralized work, taking advantage of this technology, will be more focused on self-organizing work groups to carry out specific tasks rather than being done through large organizations.

There is no question that this decentralization and moving to smaller organizations is possible, but the process of getting there will require major changes in the work environment with regard to health and medical benefits, as well as dealing with job security. People have demonstrated their great preference for job security and for less freedom of choice (and potentially lower incomes) in the past, and this human characteristic does not look likely to disappear.

While there does not seem to be any inherent reason why job growth overall would decline due to computerization of the workplace or other technological advances, since it has not declined in the past, there is also no unassailable way to disprove that "this time it is different." The important issue for our discussion is that it does not matter whether or not future job prospects will be reduced due to technological development – or other causes – this time. We proceed under the assumption that it is not due to less demand for work that the four-day workweek is desirable, but rather that it should be considered as a superior use of time. So if demand for work were in fact to decline in the future, this would strengthen our case, but our argument is that the four-day workweek is desirable as an improvement on individual time use and life satisfaction, rather than a measure to deal with unemployment.

CONCLUSIONS

Technology is a threatening challenge to jobs and has been since the dawn of the Industrial Revolution 300 years ago. In fact, one could point to technology changes much further back in history that upset the social order, such as hunter–gatherer societies moving into farming and more settled lifestyles. Hunters were replaced by farmers; jobs were needed in preparing the food produced on farms for consumption and for trading to exchange products produced on different farms. Another example of technology change that greatly affected society was the domestication of the horse several thousand years ago. This change enabled people to travel greater distances and opened up trade in that way; it enabled farmers to plow much greater-sized fields; and it revolutionized warfare with horsemen and chariots on the battlefield. Jobs changes due to the introduction of domesticated horses were numerous and across many sectors of employment. The 19th-century Luddites were not the only group of people who were opposed to technology change that disrupted social conditions in their society!

The main lesson to be drawn from this discussion is that from all technology changes in the past, new jobs were created and more employment overall has followed. Old jobs have often faded away and been replaced by machines or by other activities, but the overall job panorama has not demonstrated any tendency to shrink in size.

A real challenge today relates to the current set of technology changes in mechanizing more activities with machines, including robots, and in dealing with human bodies through biotech that extends lives and repairs body ailments. These major changes are creating new jobs, eliminating old ones, and altering the social structure by extending people's lives. The problem of replacing jobs with machines is not new, though the specific jobs and machines may be. This challenge has been successfully dealt with in the past, and optimists see no reason to expect a different outcome this time.

The fact that people are living longer and that society overall is aging presents another set of challenges that have not been dealt with before. New living arrangements and new jobs for senior citizens (say, over 60 years old) are needed, and social adjustment is needed to incorporate these people into active life.

Finally, an issue that has not been discussed above is the concern about what to do to help the people who are displaced by machines (or by imports). The US does not have a policy response to the challenge of unemployment for people who are laid off due to auto-mation, though unemployment insurance does exist for a period of time after a layoff, and some subsidized training support is likewise available. For loss of jobs due to imports, there is a support program called Trade Adjustment Assistance to pay for those who are laid off to obtain training (and financial support during the training) to find jobs in other kinds of activity. Retraining auto workers to become computer programmers or health care workers or to enter hospitality management is the kind of training that is available.

A huge challenge to this retraining effort is that people have demonstrated a marked lack of willingness to move to where job opportunities exist. So, even if someone is retrained to take a job in computer programming, if the jobs are located somewhere requiring a move to a different home/apartment, etc., Americans have very often not been willing to move. This problem is beyond our current scope of analysis, but it is extremely relevant to discussions about the flexibility of the workforce to adapt to new conditions.

APPENDIX

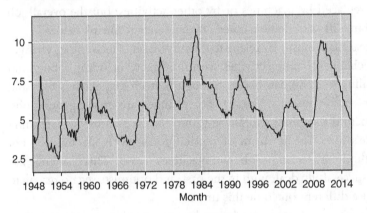

Appendix A6.1 Historical Unemployment Rate in the US

Source: US Department of Labor, Bureau of Labor Statistics, http://data.bls.gov/timeseries/LNS14000000.

NOTES

1 In fact, according to the International Encyclopedia of the Social Sciences, "Machines were not the only, or even the major, threat to the textile workers of the Midlands and North. The Prince Regent's Orders in Council, barring trade with Napoleonic France and nations friendly to France, cut off foreign markets for the British textile industry. Even more importantly, high food prices required more of each laborer's shrinking wages" www.encyclopedia.com/topic/Luddites.aspx.

2 For details on the Luddite uprising, see, for example, Bailey (1998).

3 This shift in production from cottages to factories did reduce the role of skilled weavers, but it increased overall manufacturing employment greatly. See, for

example, www.bl.uk/georgian-britain/articles/the-industrial-revolution. Also see www.historylearningsite.co.uk/britain-1700-to-1900/industrial-revolution/factories-in-the-industrial-revolution/.

4 An earlier example, taken from Frey and Osborne (2013, Footnote 9) illustrates this point in more detail: "The production of plows nicely illustrates the differences between the artisan shop and the factory. In one artisan shop, two men spent 118 man-hours using hammers, anvils, chisels, hatchets, axes, mallets, shaves and augers in 11 distinct operations to produce a plow. By contrast, a mechanized plow factory employed 52 workers performing 97 distinct tasks, of which 72 were assisted by steam power, to produce a plow in just 3.75 man-hours. The degree of specialization was even greater in the production of men's white muslin shirts. In the artisan shop, one worker spent 1439 hours performing 25 different tasks to produce 144 shirts. In the factory, it took 188 man-hours to produce the same quantity, engaging 230 different workers performing 39 different tasks, of which more than half required steam power. The workers involved included cutters, turners and trimmers, as well as foremen and forewomen, inspectors, errand boys, an engineer, a fireman, and a watchman (US Department of Labor, 1899)".

5 Even before the Luddites, there were episodes of violent reaction against machines replacing people in the workplace. Mantoux (1928, p. 409 ff.) notes the destruction of a steamboat by boatmen in Fulda in 1707 and the smashing of Jaquard's power loom in Lyons in 1801, as well as quite a few additional violent actions by workers against mechanized textile equipment.

6 See Woirol (1996, Chapter 3).

7 See US Department of Labor, Bureau of Labor Statistics, http://data.bls.gov/timeseries/LNS14000000.

8 All data from the Bureau of Labor Statistics website, www.bls.gov/data/.

9 See, for example, Bureau of Labor Statistics, www.bls.gov/opub/mlr/1986/06/art1full.pdf and www.bls.gov/news.release/archives/empsit_01072011.pdf.

10 The issue of US job losses because of Chinese manufacturing imports is a major issue. See, for example, Autor (2013).

REFERENCES

Akst, D. (2013). "What Can We Learn from Past Anxiety over Automation?" The Wilson Quarterly, Summer, http://wilsonquarterly.com/stories/theres-much-learn-from-past-anxiety-over-automation/.

Autor, D., D. Dorn, and G. Hanson (2013). "The China Syndrome: Local Labor Market Effects of Import Competition in the United States", American Economic Review. Vol. 103, 2121–2168.

Autor, D.H. (2015a). "Why Are There Still So Many Jobs? The History and Future of Workplace Automation", Journal of Economic Perspectives. Vol. 29, pp. 3–30.

Autor, D.H. (2015b). "Polanyi's Paradox and the Shape of Employment Growth", in Re-Evaluating Labor Market Dynamics. Kansas City: Federal Reserve Bank of Kansas City, pp. 129–179.

Autor, D.H., L.F. Katz, and M.S. Kearney (2006). "The Polarization of the US Labor Market", *American Economic Review Papers and Proceedings*. Vol. 96, pp. 189–194.

Bessen, J. (2015). "Toil and Technology", *Finance & Development*. Vol 52, pp. 16–19.

Bailey, B.J. (1998). *The Luddite Rebellion*. New York: New York University Press.

Brynjolfsson, E. and A. McAfee (2014). *The Second Machine Age: Work, Progress, and Prosperity in a Time of Brilliant Technologies*. New York and London: W.W. Norton & Company.

Frey, C.B. and M.A. Osborne (2013). *The Future of Employment: How Susceptible are Jobs to Computerization?* Oxford: Oxford Martin School.

Goos, M., A. Manning, and A. Salomons (2014). "Explaining Job Polarization: Routine-Biased Technological Change and Offshoring", *American Economic Review*. Vol. 104, pp. 2509–2526.

Mantoux, P. (1928). *The Industrial Revolution in the Eighteenth Century*. London: Jonathan Cape.

McAfee, A. and E. Brynjolfsson (2017). *Machine, Platform, Crowd: Harnessing our Digital Future*. New York: W.W. Norton.

Michaels, G., A. Natraj, and J. Van Reenen (2014). "Has ICT Polarized Skill Demand? Evidence from Eleven Countries over 25 Years", *The Review of Economics and Statistics*. Vol. 96, pp. 60–77.

National Commission on Technology, Automation, and Economic Progress (1966). *Technology and the American Economy*, http://files.eric.ed.gov/fulltext/ED023803.pdf.

O'Rourke, K.H., A.S. Rahman, and A.M. Taylor (2013). "Luddites, the Industrial Revolution, and the Demographic Transition", *Journal of Economic Growth*. Vol. 18, pp. 373–409.

Ross, A. (2016). *The Industries of the Future*. New York: Simon & Schuster.

Woirol, G. (1996). *The Technological Unemployment and Structural Unemployment Debates*. Westport, CT: Greenwood Press.

Seven

To restate the central proposition: why not reduce the number of work days to four per week from five per week, with hours per day remaining the same? This would give everyone (who could structure work this way) 20% more time for leisure and other activities.[1] So, how could this be accomplished, starting from today's standard of a five-day, 40-hour workweek?

Fundamentally, the change would take place by making one more day into a weekend day, say Friday. Then office and factory and other wage-earning workers would put in eight-hour days on Monday through Thursday. (Professional and managerial people would work four-day weeks as well, though their hours would not be limited to 32 per week just as they are not limited to 40 per week now.) The typical office would be open for business during normal hours on Monday through Thursday and closed during Friday through Sunday.

As far as the production of goods and services is concerned, this subject was initially discussed in Chapter 3. The results of previous workweek reductions in the US included significant increases in hourly output with initial declines in overall weekly output. Over time the (slightly) reduced output was recouped, and the economy returned to its previous growth path. This means that, everything else being equal, a loss of one day of the workweek would initially reduce output somewhat – and potentially reduce worker incomes by that same per-centage, unless different conditions were negotiated.

This is really a silly counterfactual view, since freeing up one more day a week would result in people spending more money on leisure activities, working second jobs, and generally replacing lost GDP with new activities that produce income for the society overall. It does not imply that the new total GDP for the country would be the same as before, but it definitely would not just drop by 20%. The overall impact will depend on how much productivity increases, how much wages and salaries are reduced, and how much additional activity is generated during the long weekend.

The impacts of this shift to the four-day workweek will be different depending on the type of work involved. Private sector and government offices that are open from nine to five during Monday to Friday today would just reduce the number of days that they offer services to the public from five to four per week. Hotels that are open every day with long hours of availability of most services would continue to operate seven days a week, but they would staff their facilities with a quarter more people to replace the eight hours per week lost from the existing employees. Other kinds of business or activity would require other kinds of adjustments, as discussed in more detail below.

BUSINESSES/OFFICES THAT ARE OPEN 40 HOURS, 5 DAYS PER WEEK

There are a variety of ways to deal with the complications here if we remain focused on an office or a production facility that will be closed one more day per week than before. Perhaps most importantly, for those workers who want to retain their previous incomes, assuming no change in hourly compensation, there would be a need to offer them two additional hours per day of work (from Monday through Thursday). So, the schedule of the business would have to be adjusted from perhaps from nine to five to eight to six in order to accommodate those people. This implies more complications, since not all functions would be feasible to offer during the additional hours unless sufficient numbers of workers chose to remain at 40 hours per workweek. That is, if the business were open two more hours per day, that would require adequate staffing to provide the products/services sold to clients; and the people who, by their own preference, choose to work those additional hours may not have the optimal distribution of skills needed, so some staffing complications will likely remain during those hours.[2] The important element is that the office/factory/business would remain closed on Friday through Sunday instead of just Saturday through Sunday. And over time, it is expected that more and more people will choose to work the 32 hours, so that there will be less demand for the overtime during the four workdays per week.

It is certain that some inconveniences will arise when some services are not available on Fridays rather than just on Saturdays and Sundays. Initially, there will be complaints about inadequate service, which will have to be managed in some way. Perhaps some specific services could be made available on Fridays, with appropriate assignment of staffing for that purpose.[3] One of the attractive features of cutting out Friday work is that the office or production facility can be closed on that day, so having some service(s) still provided on Fridays would complicate this feature. And if the office is closed on Friday, that means no commuting problems for those employees and no operational costs for those offices, except fixed costs.

RESTAURANTS/HOTELS/BUSINESSES THAT ARE ALREADY OPEN FOR EXTENDED HOURS, SAY SEVEN DAYS A WEEK

For a business that already uses shift work to accommodate a longer-than-40-hour workweek, there will likely be no major challenges. Instead of finding sufficient staff working 40 hours per week for the various services offered every day of the week, the business will need to hire more people to fill in the hours freed up by those who move to a 32-hour workweek. If the workers originally worked five eight-hour days, then a new worker will be needed for every four existing workers in order to offer services during the same hours.

Companies that operate six or seven days per week, such as retail stores, hospitals, hotels, restaurants, and many more service businesses, will not be able to close for three days per week. They already face this problem even with a 40-hour workweek, and they have to assign employees to work schedules that overlap in order to provide customer service during extended hours and weekends. Think of staffing at stores such as Walmart or restaurants such as McDonald's, where scheduling requires three to four times the number of total employees as the number on duty at any time, to deal with 7 a.m. to 10 p.m. or 6 a.m. to midnight operating hours in the stores or restaurants. The scheduling challenge would just require more employees to be spread over these seven days per week schedules. Table 7.1 illustrates this scheduling problem, which is really just a linear programming problem subject to simple constraints.

Table 7.1 How to Schedule the Reduced Workweek

Feasible Staffing with a 5-day Workweek

	Monday	Tuesday	Wednesday	Thursday	Friday	Saturday	Sunday
6 a.m.–10 a.m.	P1, P3, P5, P9, P11	P1, P3, P7, P9, P11	P1, P3, P7, P9, P13	P1, P5, P7, P9, P13	P1, P5, P7, P11, P13	P3, P5, P7, P11, P13	P3, P5, P9, P11, P13
10 a.m.–2 p.m.	P1, P3, P5, P9, P11	P1, P3, P7, P9, P11	P1, P3, P7, P9, P13	P1, P5, P7, P9, P13	P1, P5, P7, P11, P13	P3, P5, P7, P11, P13	P3, P5, P9, P11, P13
2 p.m.–6 p.m.	P2, P4, P6, P10, P12	P2, P4, P8, P10, P12	P2, P4, P8, P10, P14	P2, P6, P8, P10, P14	P2, P6, P8, P12, P14	P4, P6, P8, P12, P14	P4, P6, P10, P12, P14
6 p.m.–10 p.m.	P2, P4, P6, P10, P12	P2, P4, P8, P10, P12	P2, P4, P8, P10, P14	P2, P6, P8, P10, P14	P2, P6, P8, P12, P14	P4, P6, P8, P12, P14	P4, P6, P10, P12, P14

Assuming the need for five workers at work at all times; 14 total workers are needed. This could be a hotel or a restaurant, for example. P1: person 1, etc.

Feasible Staffing with a Four-day Workweek

	Monday	Tuesday	Wednesday	Thursday	Friday	Saturday	Sunday
6 a.m.–10 a.m.	P1, P3, P7, P11, P15	P1, P5, P7, P11, P15	P1, P5, P9, P11, P15	P1, P5, P9, P13, P15	P3, P5, P9, P13, P17	P3, P7, P9, P13, P17	P3, P7, P11, P13, P17
10 a.m.–2 p.m.	P1, P3, P7, P11, P15	P1, P5, P7, P11, P15	P1, P5, P9, P11, P15	P1, P5, P9, P13, P15	P3, P5, P9, P13, P17	P3, P7, P9, P13, P17	P3, P7, P11, P13, P17
2 p.m.–6 p.m.	P2, P4, P8, P12, P16	P2, P6, P8, P12, P16	P2, P6, P10, P12, P16	P2, P6, P10, P14, P16	P4, P6, P10, P14, P18	P4, P8, P10, P14, P18	P4, P8, P12, P14, P18
6 p.m.–10 p.m.	P2, P4, P8, P12, P16	P2, P6, P8, P12, P16	P2, P6, P10, P12, P16	P2, P6, P10, P14, P16	P4, P6, P10, P14, P18	P4, P8, P10, P14, P18	P4, P8, P12, P14, P18

Assuming the need for five workers at all times; a minimum of 18 workers are needed, with the last two workers only assigned 24 hours (three days) of work per week. This problem could be finessed with part-time workers. P1: person 1, etc.

This staffing assignment chart would vary depending on how many workers are needed at any time. If the needs vary during the week, this would change the assignments. If more or less than five workers are needed, this would change the assignments. In sum, these charts are just illustrative of the planning challenge of fitting multiple workers into time slots through a week longer than four days and with more than eight daily hours of coverage. The example assumes that all employees require the same skills, so that managers and other skill-specific employees would require additional scheduling programs.

Table 7.1 shows a workplace that is open from 6 a.m. to 10 p.m., seven days a week. Staffing for this workplace requires five people on duty at all times. This means that the company would have to have 14 employees (managers not included) who work five days and eight hours per day, as shown in the first panel of Table 7.1.

If the workweek were reduced to four days of eight hours of work, this workplace would need 18 employees to cover the week, as shown in the second panel of Table 7.1. And the week would be complicated by the fact that the last two workers would only be needed for three days per week, essentially working part-time. In the hotel/restaurant/retail store context, this need for part-time workers would not be particularly challenging, since it is commonly done already. For both the four-day and five-day workweeks, managers would have to be assigned to oversee the operation, and this would certainly require an additional manager(s) working a four-day week. The challenge to managers is not really different from that facing other employees, since the company will have to have more than one manager working each day to handle the 16-hour workday and more than one additional manager to cover a seven-day workweek when the four-day workweek is implemented. It is just another linear programming problem for managerial employees.

If reduced work hours indeed produce less output (even with the expected increase in productivity due to greater motivation/vitality of the workforce), then companies will need to hire additional employees to fill in the time required to produce their products and services. This will add to the current level of employment (or reduce unemployment, if you look at it from that perspective). Think about a retail store that is open every day of the week (e.g., grocery stores, mall stores, restaurants). Creating a four-day, 32-hour workweek for the employees means that the stores will lose 20% of the work time that existing employees provide. So they will have to hire 25% more people to perform the regular tasks that are needed to operate these stores.[4]

Once again, the workers may choose to retain their existing wages and continue to work 40 hours per week, thus not requiring additional staff. For those workers who accept the 32-hour workweek, their final eight hours will be filled by a new person, and the compensation for those hours will be paid to that person. Given that productivity is expected to rise with the shorter workweek, it may be possible for the company to offer its workers higher hourly wages to partially compensate for the reduced hours. It is not clear if increased productivity and increased wages, plus some new workers, will yield a net zero impact on employer costs, but it may be reasonably close to that outcome. This is really an empirical question that has to be answered when the change is made, leaving some risk that employer costs may rise somewhat.

SCHOOLS/COLLEGES/UNIVERSITIES

Schools and universities would also face a challenge with the reduced number of "normal" teaching days. Universities could cope well by scheduling typically twice per week 1.5-hour classes on Monday plus Wednesday and Tuesday plus Thursday – though this would put a strain on science labs that are already booked for all five days and other similar facility uses. The school year could be adjusted slightly as well, in case one or two more weeks of class might be needed to fulfill teaching/learning hour requirements.[5]

Elementary schools and high schools would face the challenge of adding 1.5 hours per day of instructional time, so that the number of legally required credit hours could still be met. This would tax the students and the teachers to stay alert and motivated for that extra time – even though the longer weekends would allow for plenty of rest! Teachers would be faced with probably more grading during the shorter workweek, but then rewarded with more days of non-teaching at the weekend every week as well. The number of teaching/learning hours would not change, but it might cause teachers to shift more of their grading and preparation time to the (longer) weekends. Based on state education requirements concerning minimum hours of instruction (in the US today, about 990 hours per year[6]), it might be necessary to extend the school year by a week or two – just as with universities. Probably some combination of a slightly longer school day and an extra week or two added to the school year would work most effectively.

The implications for extracurricular activities should not be ignored here. If sports and arts activities are carried out after school, then the timing of these activities would be affected by a longer school day. If the "normal" school day includes 5.5 hours per day of instruction, then that implies $5.5 \times 5 = 27.5$ hours per week, not including breaks. This could be accomplished in four days with a seven-hour instructional day – or in four days with somewhat fewer hours (say 6.5 hours) along with a slightly longer school year. It is easy to speculate here about how manageable the longer school day would be, but for the teachers who are also coaches or arts instructors after school, the workday could be very long indeed.

It is likely that teachers would oppose the shift to a four-day workweek for the reasons just noted. A longer workday does not sound attractive, even with a three-day weekend. A slightly longer school year likewise would require the teachers to adjust their summer plans slightly. Because it would be a change in the status quo and because many schoolteachers are unionized, there likely would be labor pressure against the change, even if the outcome would ultimately prove to be beneficial and attractive to the teachers once they experience it. For these reasons, it seems likely that primary and secondary education may lag in the shift to a four-day workweek. Universities would not necessarily face the same level of resistance, though some real obstacles such as running all or most classes on the Monday plus Wednesday and Tuesday plus Thursday schedule and also scheduling laboratory use will need to be overcome.

DOCTORS, LAWYERS, AND OTHER PROFESSIONALS

Individuals who work as sole proprietors or as experts/professionals in a business such as accounting or medicine will have a straightforward choice. If they move to a four-day workweek, they can instantly accommodate the new model at a reduced income level. If they want to maintain hours and billing, they certainly could expand the workday on the remaining four working days of the week, or they could choose some intermediate step such as extending their hours by one hour per day and still reduce the overall workweek by four hours (and one day) per week. This intermediate step would still imply somewhat lower earnings for the individual, unless he/she could increase productivity by accommodating more clients per hour during the four days.

This situation is perhaps mitigated by the fact that today many or most physicians, lawyers, accountants, and other such professionals work in groups, ranging from giant law firms and the Big 4 accounting firms to group medical and dental practices. Given that they are operating in organizations with multiple providers of their services, these professionals can readily switch to the 32-hour, four-day work-week and just allow the remaining workload to be assigned to new hires in those firms/organizations. And those who prefer to maintain their existing hours can presumably work ten-hour days for the four workdays of the week.

The critical element here as elsewhere is that the law firms, doctors' offices, accounting firms, etc., must be open to the public just four days a week, like other offices and manufacturing firms. If they shifted the workload to a five-day schedule with added staffing, this would defeat a key purpose of the four-day workweek, which is to create a three-day weekend. And managers in these organizations would lose, because they would still be needed for the five days that the office was open each week. To benefit from the four-day workweek, the doctors and lawyers and others would need to offer just four days of service to the public per week.

MANAGERS AND OTHER SALARIED EMPLOYEES

The 32-hour, four-day workweek structure is not feasible across all forms of employment equally. Hourly workers can easily be shifted into one less day per week, with new people hired to fill in that gap. Salaried – or white-collar, exempt, or whatever other label is used to imply jobs that do not have a fixed time schedule – people would face a different challenge. As long as the workweek is defined as Monday through Thursday, then they would be able to have the same weekend as the hourly workers who are moving from Monday through Friday to the shorter week. If their work were spread over five days and workers were spread over the five days to accomplish the 32-hour workweek for workers, then the salaried people would not necessarily benefit at all from a shorter workweek, because their workdays were probably more than eight hours before the change anyway. So to benefit man-agerial and professional people, the plan would necessarily have to define which days of the week constitute the "normal" four-day work-week and add the extra day to the weekend.[7]

Restaurants and hotels that are open six or seven days per week have long ago resolved this challenge by employing assistant man-agers who take responsibility for overseeing the business during weekends (or whichever two days per week the manager is off). An assistant manager could serve in any business that chose or needed to operate more than four days per week, leaving the manager and workers to the four-day workweek. It is fundamental to the four-day workweek that the standard week is indeed four days so that weekends can be redesigned by individuals to fit the new three-day weekend regime.

THE FINANCIAL CHALLENGE

Who will pay for the loss of a fifth of the workweek when people move to a four-day workweek? This subject was discussed in Chapter 5 above, so it will not be revisited here in detail, except to note that there is a cost to reducing the hours worked per week, and that cost has to be shouldered by someone. What appears to be the simplest option is for workers to take the 20% pay cut in exchange for a 20% workload reduction, and then allow them to recoup the loss over time with wage increases related to productivity gains. It has been shown that hourly productivity increases with the reduction in work hours, so that will absorb some of the loss of output (e.g., Golden 2012). For the purpose of our discussion, we will assume that 10% (i.e., half of 20%) of the lost hours is replaced by increased productivity. This is not inconsistent with the empirical findings in previous worktime reductions, and it is in fact a conservative estimate. Given this assumption, the wage reduction would be 10%, which is a much more tolerable amount in exchange for the extra day off.

In previous studies, it has been shown that wage increases follow workload reductions as firms compete for scarce human resources (e.g., Askenazy 2013). While this wage increase would reduce company profitability, it would also tend to lead to less demand for labor and a move toward a situation in which companies employ relatively fewer new employees, while retaining the existing ones for fewer hours per week. This is one of the reasons that it is not possible to just say that reducing hours for existing workers will increase employment by 20% to cover the lost time.

At the same time, workers should be permitted to continue at 40 hours per week, just working the last eight hours as overtime (with no surcharge added onto those extra hours). This will enable those who wish to keep their current earnings to do so, with the expectation that over a few years everyone will get used to the 32-hour workweek, and people will accept the shorter workweek along with the compensation that will soon recoup the original level.

Alternatives to this simplest scheme would be arrangements such as having companies accept an initial hit in earnings by dropping wages by less than 20% and then catching up later with lower pay raises than normal for a few years. While this is not precisely what Henry Ford did in 1926, he did achieve a one-day-shorter workweek with the company taking the financial hit. He found that productivity really jumped with the new arrangement, so the financial burden was much less than 20% of wages paid; in fact, it was claimed that Ford produced as many cars in five days per week as it had previously in six days per week.[8] Workers did not have to accept a pay cut, and Ford probably gained significantly by reducing the likelihood of strike activity that tended to plague auto manufacturing in that era.[9]

WHO JUMPS FIRST?

Even assuming that the principle of the 32-hour, four-day workweek is acceptable to many, how will it enter into operation? The government certainly could be the instigator, but as we have seen with past episodes of change in the workweek, it has come either through workers' efforts protesting harsh working conditions (i.e., strikes, protests [including violent ones], etc.) or through unilateral company moves, such as Ford Motor Company's switch to the 40-hour workweek. Someone has to be the leading actor, and governments are not likely candidates for such a role.

It might make sense for some high-tech company(ies) such as Google and Apple or the members of the Semiconductor Industry Association to launch the four-day workweek, since they are at the vanguard of work in the 21st-century US. Or it could be an iconic business leader similar to Jack Welch (retired from General Electric) or Sam Walton (deceased founder of Walmart); it could be another auto magnate such as Mary Barra (CEO of General Motors), or the iconic investor/portfolio manager Warren Buffett of Berkshire Hathaway. It could even be Ford Motor Company again – just think of the fantastic publicity the company would receive for taking this bold step.[10]

Once the first company or companies make the move, a large demonstration effect will follow, as with the Ford Motor Company move in 1926. Other companies will come under pressure from workers to match the leader's policy, and surely some will jump on the bandwagon just to be in the vanguard of such change. There is no assurance that the reduced workweek will sweep the economy overnight, but in the fast-moving 21st century, it is very likely that it will not take 12 years for the government to consolidate the change, as it did with the Fair Labor Standards Act of 1938[11] that formalized the 40-hour workweek for employees in companies involved in inter-state commerce.

ADJUSTMENT COSTS

When the four-day workweek is established, there will undoubtedly be adjustment costs, from dealing with changes in people's incomes and daily habits to complications arising from the fact that not all businesses will implement the new schedule at the same time. While these complications do make the transition period somewhat more costly than "business as usual," they should not be viewed as cause for derailing the process.

The income question has been discussed fairly extensively in Chapter 5 as well as above in the current chapter. There is no doubt that workers should expect lower compensation for the 20% fewer hours worked. However, as discussed above, the previous experiences with workload reductions have produced significant productivity gains, so that worker incomes should not suffer more than perhaps a 10% reduction. And of course anyone who wished to avoid income reduction could simply work "overtime" hours to maintain their current income. Assuming the productivity gains noted, this would require about four extra hours per week, or four nine-hour days instead of eight-hour days.

If schools do not initially move to the four-day schedule, then parents will be faced with the complication that they will need to provide transportation to school for their children until the school week is adjusted – which could be several years. Even so, this should not be complicated, since existing transportation should still remain in effect until schools undertake the schedule change. The only way that parents would be affected significantly is if they work overtime during the four-day workweek and then encounter complications with getting their children to school because of their own new, longer schedules on those four days.

The clash between those whose jobs move to four days per week and those whose organizations do not move to the new schedule will certainly cause frictions. A husband whose job moves to four days per week will find sharing transport to work difficult with a wife whose job remains at five days per week, at least on the one day of difference. More clashes may be anticipated between those who are freed up for the extra day each week and those who are not.

Despite these concerns, it should be noted that for all of the services and product companies that have multiple shifts already, the new workweek will simply cause an adjustment of shift assignments and no change in services offered, so the adjustment costs will be minimal. Thus, hotels, restaurants, mall stores, etc., will not demonstrate any change in hours open to the public, but they will need to increase staffing as employees will individually work fewer hours per week. The situation would be similar for factories that operate more than one eight-hour shift per day; no change in production need occur, but staffing will have to be increased.

EXAMPLES

There are quite a few examples of companies that have moved to a four-day, 32-hour workweek. Almost all of them are small. Tech start-ups such as Basecamp and SchooLinks in the US have implemented the four-day workweek, but they employ in total about 100 people. Large-scale examples of moving to a four-day (compressed) workweek include the Government of the State of Utah, which implemented a 40-hour workweek over four days in 2008, only to discontinue the program within three years.

The example of the French legislation establishing a 35-hour workweek in 1998 and launched in 2000, discussed in Chapter 2, remains as probably the largest-scale reduced-hours workweek on record today. And in Sweden in 2016, a push to implement a six-hour workday was undertaken and implemented in a few companies and in the city of Gothenburg, but it was not widely accepted and has been largely discontinued.[12] Both of these European examples have aimed at reducing the length of the workday without creating an extra weekend day.

CONCLUSIONS

The move to a four-day, 32-hour workweek is quite feasible in the early 21st century. The workweek has not formally changed since the 1920s, even though actual hours worked in most countries have declined to something less than 40 hours of work per week today. The adjustment to the shorter workweek will have different implications for different kinds of income-earning activity. Offices and businesses that work on a five-day schedule could switch to the four-day schedule simply in the broad sense of just dropping one workday per week, though the details could still be complicated. Businesses that already operate on extended schedules beyond 40 hours per week will just need additional staffing to cope with the change.

A key issue that needs to be emphasized is that no one would be forced to switch to a 32-hour workweek if he/she chose not to, so the opportunity for people to work "overtime" to recoup the eight hours per week that are dropped needs to be offered. In some kinds of business this might be complicated (i.e., operating beyond eight hours per day to accommodate those who want to maintain 40 hours of work per week). It is expected that over a few years people would become accustomed to the four-day workweek and it would be accepted as the norm.

The critical need is for some large employer to move first and to demonstrate the benefits of the 32-hour workweek. This could most likely be a large company or industry group. Some industrialist who wants to demonstrate forward-looking leadership could be the one to do this. Or it could be a self-interested businessperson, as arguably Henry Ford was, who expects that workers will be greatly motivated to work for his/her company under the new schedule because it offers so much more flexibility in the week. Ford was able to both quell labor unrest in the auto industry and generate a very benevolent public appearance for the company. Employee satisfaction and public perception of a company are still major goals of businesses today.

The four-day, 32-hour workweek can be implemented if a strong and credible leader takes the reins and makes the bold move. In that sense, "where there's a will, there's a way." The key problem is to find the will to start things going. Small tech companies such as Basecamp, iBeat, and SchooLinks have made the move without influencing other companies or communities to endorse the concept. One giant will make the difference.

NOTES

1 Compensation schemes (see Chapter 5) are needed to deal with this change, but the logic is that we don't need to be producing ever more things while the number of consumers of those things is not growing. This is true for the Triad countries and for many more countries in the world, including China. However, global population is expected to continue to grow for another 20–30 years before stabilizing or beginning to decline. See, for example, www.slate.com/articles/technology/future_tense/2013/01/world_population_may_actually_start_declining_not_exploding.html.

2 Another likely outcome is that some people will accept the 32-hour workweek and then go out and seek a second job for one or more days per week to thus supplement their incomes and use some of the additional available time.

3 When the State of Utah tried a four-day workweek in 2008, people complained about the lack of driver's license facilities on Fridays. So, the state opened facilities for this purpose on Fridays, as an exception to the general closing of state offices on those days. See, for example, Facer and Wadsworth (2010, p. 1043).

4 Companies will have to hire 25% more people to replace the ones who move to 32 hours per weeks. For every four people who switch to a 32hour workweek, $4 \times 8 = 32$ hours of replacement work is needed, or one more employee.

5 A friend of mine who is a university president points out that the main problem in moving to a four-day workweek will be to push the notoriously stubborn professors to accept the change, when they generally have the ability to resist changes in their working conditions. This could be a real challenge!

6 This 990 hour school year was the minimum allowed in New York, Virginia, Massachusetts, and more than 30 other states in 2016.

7 Just as the original move from a six-day workweek to a five-day workweek in the late 1800s selected Saturday as the added vacation day because it is the Jewish Sabbath, it would make sense to add Friday to the weekend for a four-day work-week, because Friday is the Islamic Jum'a (the Islamic equivalent of Sabbath).

8 For citations, see www.pbs.org/livelyhood/workday/weekend/laborhistorian.html.

9 Henry Ford's Detroit-based automobile company had broken ground in its labor policies before. In early 1914, against a backdrop of widespread unemployment and increasing labor unrest, Ford announced that it would pay its male factory workers a minimum wage of $5 per eight-hour day, upped from a previous rate of $2.34 for nine hours (the policy was adopted for female workers in 1916). The news shocked many in the industry – at the time, $5 per day was nearly double what the average auto worker made – but it turned out to be a stroke of brilliance, immediately boosting productivity along the assembly line and building a sense of company loyalty and pride among Ford's workers (www.history.com/this-day-in-history/ford-factory-workers-get-40-hour-week).

10 As nice at this idea is to have Ford lead once again, the desirable leader would probably be a new-economy company such as Google or Amazon, since they are emblematic of the 21st century. Another example of such leadership was J.P.

Morgan himself in the Panic of 1893 and the Panic of 1907, as well as his bank in the Depression, when Morgan and led the financial industry in providing financing and stopping the panics. JPMorgan Chase performed a similar role under Jamie Dimon during the Global Financial Crisis in 2008–9 when it acquired the failing Bear Stearns investment bank in March 2008 and later the failing savings bank Washington Mutual in September 2008.

11 See the Fair Labor Standards Act, www.dol.gov/whd/regs/statutes/ FairLaborStandAct.pdf.

12 See, for example, BBC (2017). "What really happened when Swedes tried six-hour days?", www.bbc.com/news/business-38843341. See also Alderman (2016).

REFERENCES

Alderman, L. (2016). "In Sweden, an Experiment Turns Shorter Workdays Into Bigger Gains", New York Times, May 20, www.nytimes.com/2016/05/21/business/international/in-sweden-an-experiment-turns-shorter-workdays-into-bigger-gains.html.

Askenazy, P. (2013). "Working Time Regulation in France from 1996 to 2012", Cambridge Journal of Economics. Vol. 37, pp. 323–347.

Eisenberg, R. (2015). "It's High Time for the 4-Day Workweek", Next Avenue, www.nextavenue.org/its-high-time-4-day-workweek/.

Facer, R. and L. Wadsworth (2010). "Four-Day Work Weeks: Current Research and Practice", Connecticut Law Review. Vol. 42. pp. 1031–1046.

Golden, L. (2012). "The effects of working time on productivity and firm performance: a research synthesis paper", in Conditions of Work and Employment Series No. 33. Geneva: International Labour Office.

Eight

INTRODUCTION

There is nothing sacred about a 40-hour workweek. Historically, since the beginning of the Industrial Revolution in the mid-1700s, workweeks for the production of goods and services were six days long, and hours were more than ten per day.[1] The 70- to 72-hour workweek was common, with Sunday a holiday and work going from dawn to dusk during the six workdays of the week. In agriculture, the main sector of employment in the 19th century, the workweek was probably shorter for actual work in the fields, but longer overall because of additional work needed on the farm and to provide daily food and housing needs. Unfortunately, no separate record exists for the workweek in the agriculture sector.[2] The problem is that agricultural workers were generally self-employed and they did not clearly distinguish work hours from home hours.[3] Nevertheless, workweeks were long in all sectors, covering six days per week through the 1800s and lasting from 9 to 12 hours per day.

It was only after the Civil War in the US that labor unions were able to push their interests forward with companies and with legislators, eventually achieving a ten-hour workday before the end of the century. This movement continued into the early 1900s, when workers in a number of sectors were able to obtain an eight-hour workday for the six workdays of the week.[4] And then, during the booming 1920s, unions convinced a number of employers to accept a five-day, 40-hour workweek. Ford Motor Company was one of the first to adopt this system, for its factory workers in May 1926 and for office staff in August 1926.[5] This 40-hour workweek became law in the US in 1938 with the passage of the Fair Labor Standards Act.

Very little has changed in the US since that time. Some companies implemented reduced work hours during the Depression to try to avoid layoffs. Those policies were later dropped when World War II essentially put everyone to work. After the war, organized labor focused much more on increasing health benefits, pensions, and work rules to ensure fairness, rather than on aiming to reduce the workweek. So, the 40-hour workweek survived for another century without much change, even to this day.

Today, pressure from labor aims more to try to ensure benefits that were also targets after World War II (to obtain health and welfare support through various federal programs such as Medicaid, Aid for Families with Dependent Children [now TANF, Temporary Assistance for Needy Families], and Obamacare). However, in the current climate, where organized labor is much less effective and where most people work in services rather than manufacturing or extractive sectors, labor pressure is much less. It would make sense to pursue the line of reduced work hours in the 21st century with a move to the 32-hour, four-day workweek, but individuals and labor groups have focused their attentions elsewhere.

The way to achieve the transition from 40 hours to 32 hours per workweek is not obvious. If some companies make the move, then the demonstration that this is possible and that it works will come from that experience. If the government were to impose a shorter workweek, the decision unquestionably would be attacked and probably the effort would be derailed. Just as with Henry Ford and Ford Motor Company in 1926, the change will most likely need to come from employers – and ultimately the government will be able to establish the new norm as a rule (as happened 12 years later in 1938 with the 40-hour workweek).

HISTORY FROM THE BEGINNING OF THE INDUSTRIAL REVOLUTION

The US was primarily an agricultural economy during the 18th century, even after the Industrial Revolution in England brought many workers into factories and into the manufacturing of clothing, shoes, metal and wood products, and other items that could be made on an assembly line. Records show[6] that the workweek went from Monday through Saturday, with normal hours ranging between 10 and 12 per day. This was initially not viewed as burdensome for factory workers, since the alternative was to work on farms where hours often were even longer and conditions were subject to variations in weather and geography.

Manufacturing was well underway in the US in the late 1700s. Groups of laborers were even able to put together protests against long hours and low wages, such as in New York in 1768 when a group of tailors protested a wage reduction, and in Philadelphia in 1794 when a group of shoemakers formed a guild or union to protect their members' interests.[7] Even so, the majority of US workers remained in the agricultural sector until the late 19th century, and so average work hours were driven more by agricultural work than manufacturing.

THE 1800S

Although the US economy was still primarily agricultural during most of the 1800s, the Industrial Revolution had taken hold, and many factories and offices employed an important part of the total work force. The industrial workweek actually exceeded the agricultural one, though both were quite long by today's standards. Looking at employment in 1832, for example, Atack and Bateman (1992) found that manufacturing employees worked more than 11 hours per day, Monday through Saturday, for a total of 68 hours per week. This estimate was corroborated by evidence compiled by Weeks (1883), who found that manufacturing workers worked about 11.5 hours per day in 1832.

Dankert et al. (1965) found that by the 1840s there were several steps taken to move to a ten-hour workday (and a six-day workweek). They found evidence that artisans and mechanics had successfully achieved a ten-hour workday by the mid-1830s, though the Depression of 1837 set back that advance. President Van Buren used an executive order in 1940 to set a ten-hour workday for all employees working on government projects. This step seemed to be a major advance, but it did not filter down to companies or other organizations. According to Dankert et al. (1965), the 12-hour workday was the standard in the US until after the Civil War.

While these data refer to manufacturing employment, as shown in Appendix Table A8.2, agricultural labor by 1880 involved working about 9.5 hours per day during a six-day workweek, which was slightly less than for manufacturing workers.[8]

After the Civil War (1861–5), factory and mining labor groups formed and began pushing for lower hours and higher wages. These groups aimed either at higher wages and better treatment for their members or for lower working hours. For example, the National

Labor Union, led by Ira Steward, pushed for an eight-hour workday, six days a week – even before the ten-hour workday had been achieved on any scale in the US. The largest US labor group in the 1860s, the Knights of Labor, set their targets on labor rights and wages rather than work hours.

Some companies did reduce work hours during the post-Civil War period, but most did not. The US Government and several states set rules for an eight-hour workday in the 1860s, but these rules applied "only where there is no special contract or agreement to the contrary" (Dankert et al. 1965, p. 20). As shown in Figure 8.1, the ten-hour workday was only consolidated by 1880, and the eight-hour workday was still on a distant future horizon. Labor efforts to push for an eight-hour day resulted in the most egregious protest in 1886: in Haymarket Square in Chicago.[9] The protest against the McCormick Harvester company turned into a riot, and a dozen protesters and seven policemen were killed in the violence. After a legal trial that resulted in charging the conspirators of the riot, four of them were hung, two put in life imprisonment, and one jailed for 15 years.

In the 1890s, the labor movement and government policies both continued to push for an eight-hour workday for six days per week.

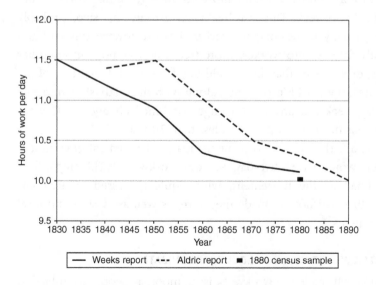

Figure 8.1 The Trend in Hours of Labor, 1830–1890
Source: Atack and Bateman (1992, p. 137).

Samuel Gompers led the newly established American Federation of Labor group of unions in pursuing this goal, along with improved working conditions, during that decade. While no major results were accomplished, the movement became widely known, understood, and supported.

THE EARLY 1900S – MAJOR CHANGES

Probably the most unexpected and large-scale change in the workweek occurred in the first 20 years of the 20th century.[10] First, several unions were able to come to agreement with employers to accept an eight-hour workday in a six-day workweek. Both steel and textile workers accomplished this step by 1923. Even before World War I, the pressure was on to reduce the workday to eight hours. Whaples (1990) argues that this was due to rapid growth of the economy, the growing strength of organized labor, government rules that promoted the eight-hour day, electrification of the manufacturing sector, and then conditions during the War when immigration declined notably. It became widely accepted at this time that factory and office workers should have a contractual workweek of 48 hours in six days.

Then in 1926 Henry Ford made his famous announcement that Ford Motor Company would move to an eight-hour workday and five-day workweek. This was really an astonishing step, probably made partially to respond to worker pressure toward this end and partially to give auto workers more free time to enjoy, among other things, driving cars that they would buy from Ford. Regardless of the reason(s), the Ford Motor policy, along with the establishment of the two-day weekend, produced a huge combined change in US work conditions in the short period of less than 20 years.

In 1938, the US Government mandated that federal government workers would have a five-day, 40-hour workweek.[11] This step effectively finalized the movement, which quickly passed on to companies that had not yet made the move, as well as to state and local governments.

AFTER WORLD WAR II – REDUCED UNIONIZATION

World War II made the workweek issue moot, as people scrambled to produce the goods and services needed for the war effort (as shown in Jones [1963] and in Appendix 8.1, the workweek rose to about 41–48 hours per week[12]). Once the war had ended, the 40-hour workweek was re-solidified and has remained in place ever since. Unions have pushed much more for better working conditions and higher wages in recent decades rather than for reduced working hours. In fact, job security may be the single most important issue on the agenda of unions and other worker organizations, since recessions in 1949, 1961, 1973–4, and 1980–2 led to nationwide concerns about joblessness. These job security concerns were continued with the dot-com crash of 2000–1 and, of course, the Global Financial Crisis of 2008–9.[13]

Organized labor has become much less of a force in US labor relations since the 1950s. In fact, union membership has declined dramatically since World War II, as manufacturing has been replaced increasingly by service sector employment. Figure 8.2 shows that

Figure 8.2 Union Membership as a Percentage of Employment in the US, 1930–2003

Source: Congressional Research Service, Union Membership Trends in the US, http://digitalcommons.ilr.cornell.edu/cgi/viewcontent. cgi?article=1176&context=key_workplace.

union membership actually peaked in the immediate post-War period, and began a steady decline in the mid-1950s. With union members only constituting about 10% of the workforce since 2000, the length of the workweek, working conditions, etc., are no longer key issues coming from that pressure group, though unions still are a vehicle for making labor issues visible as a point of national debate.

The reduction in unionization of the workforce has coincided with a noticeable increase in income inequality in the US, especially since about 1980. While this is not a central concern of our analysis, it may very well become a major issue in the years ahead. As workers perceive increasing income in the US overall, but very little increase in the incomes of those in the bottom half of the income distribution, this may provoke a backlash, ranging from protests (like Occupy Wall Street in 2011) to strikes to efforts to re-unionize the economy. While it is not clear how this might be accomplished, there does seem to be a need to enable labor to regain some degree of power in negotiating with companies in the 21st century.[14] This subject is discussed further in the conclusions in Chapter 11.

1970S – COMPRESSED WORKWEEKS

In the 1970s, perhaps partly in response to the first oil crisis in 1973–4, quite a few initiatives were launched to reduce or restructure the workweek. As discussed in Chapter 3, a number of companies and government agencies experimented with a four-day, 40-hour workweek, compressing the working hours into ten-hour days.[15]

This restructuring of the workweek did not move directly toward the goal of fewer work hours per week, but it did probe the viability of moving working time to four days per week instead of five. The experiences in the 1970s demonstrated that most people preferred the reduction in workdays to four per week, but that they eventually became less satisfied with the longer working hours during those four days. This was not a conclusive measure of the implications of a four-day workweek, but the experiences did show that people liked the extra weekend day and that they were able to accommodate the additional changes that this brought with it. The main problems were the fatigue from working long hours on the four workdays and also the complications in scheduling activities outside of the workday, such as transportation to work at earlier times and from work at later times, childcare, and other non-work activities.

SINCE 2000 – MORE FLEXIBLE WORKWEEKS

The main trends since the turn of the 21st century have been: (1) to move to more flexible work hours, so that people could configure their hours at work more adequately with their other commitments at home and elsewhere during the day; and (2) to move the work-place to the home or other sites not at the office, given the tech-nology that permits easy and inexpensive communication via Internet, phone, and other mostly electronic mechanisms. Neither of these directions relates directly to the four-day, 32-hour work-week, but they do provide alternatives to the "traditional" post-1926 workweek.

Flexible work hours

Flexible work hours have frequently been presented as a mechanism for improving the "work–life balance." However, people generally do not think of a balance between work and the rest of their lives, but rather see work as one activity and housework, leisure, education, etc., as other activities that they pursue. The "balance" does not exist because some people view work as inherently more appealing than, say, having more time for watching TV or spending more time eating or sleeping. So, flextime schedules may allow workers to assign par-ticular times of day to activities differently from a rigid nine to five, Monday to Friday schedule, but these alternatives do not necessarily lead to a different balance in overall time use.

Using the British Household Panel Survey and Understanding Society 2001–11, Wheatley (2016) found that, overall, men tended to view flexible working hours as positive and women did not. This could be attributed to women being more subject to childcare pressures and broadly more subject to more home responsibilities than men. Additional factors that contributed to preference for flex-ible work schedules were the age of the respondent (younger people preferred more flexible hours), the type of employer (public sector employees preferred flexible hours; private sector employees did not), and education level (people with less education generally preferred flexible work hours).

Another study (Eldridge and Nisar 2011) found that in a survey of about 20,000 employees in the UK, people who had flexible schedules felt more stress in their jobs, less job security, and more pressure on them to perform. These findings are almost the opposite of what one would think *a priori*, since more flexibility ought to lead to more peace of mind and more time to deal with non-work problems as they come, shifting work hours around to help people cope. However, it seemed in the study that people felt that by not following the traditional, fixed work schedule, they had to make a greater effort to demonstrate that they were contributing to the organization and not just slacking (as compared with people who were not following a flexible schedule).

So, it seems that the principle of flexible hours is quite attractive, if other things are equal. But the other things are not equal, particularly between male and female employees. Having greater flexibility in assigning one's time to work and other activities is intrinsically attractive, but the human nature of jealousy (by those who cannot take advantage of the flexibility) and gender difference (with women taking more responsibility for childcare) really make it complicated to pursue. Despite these complications, in a US Department of Labor survey in May 2012, some noteworthy characteristics of flexible worktime were found, as shown in Table 8.1.

Table 8.1 shows that about a third of US employees had flexible work hours in 2012, perhaps a surprisingly high percentage of the total workforce. The percentage has not changed much since the first survey of flexible hours in 1985, but it still constitutes a quite large part of the total workforce.

Working from Home (or Elsewhere Away from the Workplace)
Another work arrangement that has become more common in the 21st century is the use of electronic means to "commute" to work, and thus to remain at home or at least off-site to work. Many people are able to spend part of their workweek working remotely and communicating with the office/workplace through Internet, telephone, videoconference, and/or other electronic means. In some cases, the remote work is done full-time with no regular hours at the workplace. One might expect part-time remote working to offer attractive work–life flexibility and thus to be both productive

Table 8.1 Employed Persons with Flexible Work Hours by Age, Sex, Educational Attainment, and Disability Status, May 2012 (Data in Thousands)

	Total Employed	Number	Percentage of Total Employed
Total			
Total, 16 years and over	143,144	50,486	35.3
16–64 years	136,280	46,950	34.5
65 years and over	6,863	3,536	51.5
Men	75,931	27,613	36.4
Women	67,212	22,873	34
Total, 25 years and over	125,418	45,317	36.1
Less than a high school diploma	10,269	2,546	24.8
High school graduates, no college[1]	33,807	9,750	28.8
Some college or associate degree	34,398	11,857	34.5
Bachelor's degree and higher[2]	46,943	21,164	45.1
Persons with a disability			
Total, 16 years and over	5,162	2,181	42.2
16–64 years	4,350	1,716	39.4
65 years and over	812	465	57.3
Men	2,775	1,185	42.7
Women	2,387	995	41.7
Total, 25 years and over	4,829	2,089	43.3
Less than a high school diploma	576	229	39.7
High school graduates, no college[1]	1,564	572	36.6
Some college or associate degree	1,547	689	44.5
Bachelor's degree and higher[2]	1,142	600	52.6
Persons with no disability			
Total, 16 years and over	137,982	48,306	35
16–64 years	131,930	45,235	34.3
65 years and over	6,052	3,071	50.7
Men	73,156	26,428	36.1
Women	64,826	21,878	33.7
Total, 25 years and over	120,588	43,227	35.8
Less than a high school diploma	9,693	2,317	23.9
High school graduates, no college[1]	32,243	9,178	28.5
Some college or associate degree	32,851	11,168	34
Bachelor's degree and higher[2]	45,801	20,564	44.9

1 Includes persons with a high school diploma or equivalent.

2 Includes persons with Bachelor's, Master's, professional, and doctoral degrees.

Note: Flexible work hours allow employed persons to vary or make changes in the time they begin and end work.

Source: www.bls.gov/news.release/dissup.t12.htm.

and motivating. On the other hand, one could expect some level of shirking when working remotely, since there is no one to monitor performance.

Studies of this phenomenon have found fairly unambiguously that the results of remote working, at least part-time, have been positive for employer and employee. Bloom (2014) found that remote workers at the Chinese call center operator, Ctrip, were about 17% more productive and they reported much better motivation and greater commitment to the company than co-workers who worked only at the office. In their report on the US workplace, Gallup (2017) found that 43% of Americans worked partly or fully on a remote basis in 2016 compared with 39% in 2012. Likewise, the study found the 37% of people would prefer to have part of their worktime done remotely. In a 2017 report, TINYpulse consulting firm found that people working remotely felt happier at work, felt more valued at work, but felt less of a relationship with their co-workers than people working full-time at the office.

The logic of remote working seems to lead to workers feeling less stressed, more in control of their lives, and more engaged with their jobs. For companies, the use of remote workers may cut costs (since space and amenities are not needed for people who are not at the work-place) and may reduce absenteeism as well. This is a not a complete panacea, because the loss of face-to-face interaction between people does reduce the level of communication within the organization and thus leads to some inefficiencies that are overcome by working at the workplace together.

Interestingly, only about 10% of Americans worked remotely for some or all of their worktime, but for "management and professional occupations," the rate was about a third. So for the workers who are more stressed and feel more need to be face to face in the office or other workplace, the remote arrangement does not seem to be viable or available to more than perhaps 10% of them. Figure 8.3 shows the percentage of different kinds of occupations that were carried out at home over the past decade.

CONCLUSIONS

Over time, the workweek has declined dramatically, though really only after the Industrial Revolution moved people from agricultural activities

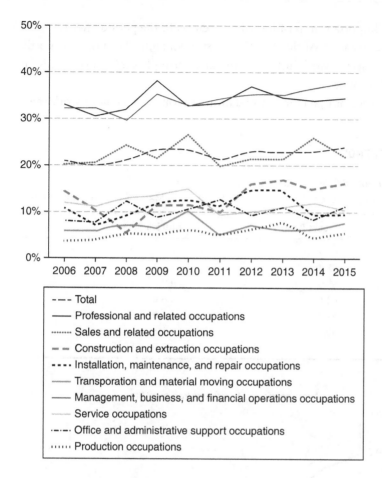

Figure 8.3 Percentage of Workers Doing Some or All of Their Work on Their Main Job at Home, 2006–2015 Annual Averages

www.bls.gov/opub/ted/2016/24-percent-of-employed-people-did-some-or-all-of-their-work-at-home-in-2015.htm.

Source: US Bureau of Labor Statistics.

into manufacturing and office work. Beginning from workweeks of 60–70+ hours per week in the 1800s, US workers dropped to 48 hours per week on average by World War I, and then to 40 hours per week after the Ford Motor policy was established in 1926. The workweek has not decreased now for about 100 years, though other workplace features have changed, such as health and safety protections, flexible worktimes, and the ability to do some work remotely. Unions were important in pushing labor agendas in the period after the Civil War until after World War II, but subsequently the move to mostly service sector work instead of manufacturing has left unions without much support.

The field is open for consideration of a four-day, 32-hour workweek.

APPENDIX

Appendix A8.1 Work Hours in the US over Time
Estimated Average Weekly Hours Worked in US Manufacturing, 1830–1990

Year	Weeks Report	Aldrich Report
1830	69.1	
1840	67.1	68.4
1850	65.5	69.0
1860	62.0	66.0
1870	61.1	63.0
1880	60.7	61.8
1890		60.0

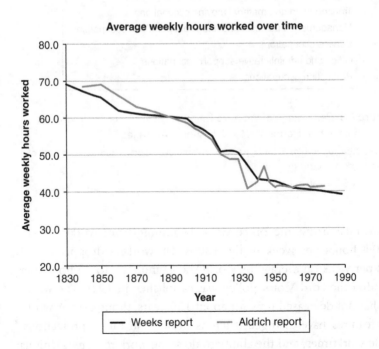

Estimated Average Weekly Hours Worked in the US, 1900–1988

Year	Census of Manufacturing	Jones Manufacturing	Owen Non-Student Males	Greis Manufacturing	Greis All Workers	Census All Workers
1900	59.6	55.0	58.5			
1904	57.9	53.6	57.1			
1909	56.8	53.1	55.7			
1914	55.1	50.1	54.0			
1919	50.8	46.1	50.0			
1924	51.1	48.8	48.8			
1929	50.6	48.0	48.7			
1934		34.4	40.6			
1940		37.6	42.5			43.3
1944		44.2	46.9			
1947		39.2	42.4	43.4	44.7	
1950		38.7	41.1			42.7
1953		38.6	41.5	43.2	44.0	
1958		37.8	40.9	42.0	43.4	
1960			41.0			40.9
1963			41.6	43.2	43.2	
1968			41.7	41.2	42.0	
1970			41.1			40.3
1973				40.6	41.0	
1978			41.3	39.7	39.1	
1980						39.8
1988						39.2

Source: Robert Whaples, "Hours of Work in U.S. History", Economic History Encyclopedia, Aug. 14, 2001, http://eh.net/encyclopedia/hours-of-work-in-u-s-history/.

Appendix A8.2 The Average Daily Scheduled Hours of Operation by Region and Industry in 1880 (Hours:Minutes)

Industry	Region				
	Midwest	Northeast	South	West	Nation
Agricultural services			9:43 (1:25)		9:45 (1:22)
Construction	9:37* (0:35)	9:42* (0:50)	9:44* (0:44)	9:40* (0:40)	9:40* (0:37)
Food	10:55* (1:39)	11:01* (1:55)	10:00 (1:35)	11:03* (1:38)	10:42* (1:48)
Tobacco	9:47*	10:00	9:51		9:53

(continued)

Appendix A8.2 (Cont.)

Industry	Region				
	Midwest	Northeast	South	West	Nation
	(0:43)	(1:00)	(0:49)		(0:52)
Textiles	10:09	9:53			10:01
	(0:39)	(0:30)			(0:39)
Clothing	9:59	10:06	10:09		10:03
	(0:40)	(1:02)	(0:45)		(0:54)
Lumber	9:58	9:59	9:46*	10:17	9:57*
	(0:48)	(0:49)	(1:03)	(0:58)	(0:53)
Furniture	9:53	9:49*	10:12		9:53*
	(0:40)	(0:36)	(1:05)		(0:43)
Paper	10:20	10:15			10:14*
	(1:00)	(1:00)			(1:01)
Printing	9:55	9:42*	9:42		9:45*
	(0:28)	(0:35)	(0:46)		(0:36)
Chemicals	10:24*	10:25*	9:53		10:16*
	(1:04)	(0:51)	(1:06)		(1:32)
Leather	10:12*	10:11*	10:16*	10:00	10:12*
	(0:52)	(0:58)	(1:20)	(0:51)	(1:01)
Glass/brick	9:48*	9:57	9:44*		9:51*
	(0:43)	(0:54)	(0:43)		(0:46)
Primary metals	9:54	9:54	9:56		9:54*
	(0:37)	(0:43)	(0:34)		(0:40)
Fabricated metals	9:45	9:52*			9:49*
	(1:00)	(0:18)			(0:39)
Machinery	9:43*	9:49*	9:49*	9:43*	9:47*
	(0:49)	(0:31)	(0:33)	(0:25)	(0:35)
Transportation equipment		9:40*			9:37*
		(0:30)			(0:33)
Miscellaneous metals	9:39*	9:55	9:54		9:52*
	(0:51)	(0:48)	(0:17)		(0:46)
Coke/gas/oil		10:37*			10:42*
		(0:48)			(0:54)
Blacksmithing	9:59	10:09*	9:58	9:40'	10:03
	(0:52)	(0:46)	(0:57)	(0:40)	(0:49)
All industries	10:05*	10:09*	9:56	10:00	10:05*
	(1:03)	(1:10)	(0:13)	(0:58)	(1:07)

* Significantly different from ten hours per day with 95% confidence.

Notes: Average hours are not given when there were insufficient observations (a minimum of 15 was required). Standard deviations are in parentheses.

Source: See Atack and Bateman (1992, p. 139, Table 1).

NOTES

1 Hellriegel (1972) noted this fact, as well as the subsequent changes in workweeks through the early 20th century. So did Atack and Bateman (1992) and Zeisel (1958).

2 Clark (2008) estimates that in 1800 farm workers had an approximately 8.2hour workday. This just included work in the fields and not additional work activity related to that.

3 See Whaples (2001) comments on the problem of measuring the agriculture workday. At least farmers did not have to commute! Since farmers tended to work at their farms, which were also their homes, it was difficult to separate out work time from non-work time.

4 Cf. Rodgers (2014, Chapter 4).

5 See, for example, www.thehenryford.org/exhibits/fmc/chrono.asp.

6 See, for example, Whaples (2001).

7 See, for example, "Labor Movement", history.com (2009), www.history.com/topics/labor.

8 This is interesting because the union movement, led visibly by Samuel Gompers, did not become a major factor in US employment until the late 1880s (as shown in the Weeks [1883] and Atack and Bateman [1992] studies), after the workweek had already dropped to six ten-hour days. The push for eight-hour days did not come until early in the 20th century.

9 The Haymarket Square riot was possibly the most important single event in US labor rights history. See, for example, www.illinoislaborhistory.org/the-haymarket-affair.

10 Whaples (1990) argues that much of the change actually occurred during the 1910–19 period, as noted in the text. However, those factors led to a six-day, 48-hour workweek. The second shoe dropped when Ford Motor Company announced a five-day, 40-hour workweek in 1926.

11 www.dol.gov/whd/regs/statutes/FairLaborStandAct.pdf.

12 See Jones (1963, p. 375).

13 One analyst stated in 2015: "The most important challenges unions from developed countries are facing today are globalization and international competition; demographic changes through migration and an ageing workforce; technological changes via elements like the sharing economy and digital innovation like automation; and the impact of climate change on jobs and the environment." See www.forbes.com/sites/kaviguppta/2016/10/12/will-labor-unions-survive-in-the-era-of-automation/#22d5bc603b22.

14 Thomas Kochan (2016, Chapters 2 and 3) examines this decline in the power of labor since the 1980s and the consequent lack of a "social contract" between labor and companies in his analysis of the future of work. While he recognizes the problem, he (and I) do not have a clear mechanism in mind to restore some kind of balance in this relationship.

15 Ronen and Primps (1981) review more than a dozen studies of the impacts and implications of the four-day, 40-hour workweek that was tried during the 1970s.

REFERENCES

Aguiar, M. and E. Hurst (2007). "Measuring Trends in Leisure: The Allocation of Time over Five Decades", *Quarterly Journal of Economics*. Vol. 122, pp. 969–1006.

Atack, J. and F. Bateman (1992). "How Long Was the Workday in 1880?", *The Journal of Economic History*. Vol. 52, pp. 129–160.

Bloom, N. (2014). "To Raise Productivity, Let More Employees Work from Home", *Harvard Business Review*. Vol. 92, pp. 28–29.

Byrd, R. (2010). "The Four-Day Work Week: Old Lessons, New Questions", *Connecticut Law Review*. Vol. 42, pp. 1059–1080.

Clark, G. (2008). *A Farewell to Alms: A Brief Economic History of the World*. Princeton, NJ: Princeton University Press.

Dankert, C.E., F.C. Mann, and H.R. Northrup (1965). *Hours of Work*. New York: Harper and Row.

Eldridge, D. and T. Nisar (2011). "Employee and Organizational Impacts of Flexitime Work Arrangements", *Relations Industrielles*. Vol. 66, pp. 213–234.

Gallup (2017). State of the American Workplace, www.gallup.com/reports/199961/state-american-workplace-report-2017.aspx.

Hellriegel, D. (1972). "The Four-Day Workweek: A Review and Assessment", *MSU Business Topics*. Vol. 20, pp. 39–47.

International Labour Organization (2007). *Working Time around the World*. New York: Routledge, www.ilo.org/wcmsp5/groups/public/@dgreports/@dcomm/@publ/documents/publication/wcms_104895.pdf.

Jones, E. (1963). "New Estimates of Hours of Work Per Week and Hourly Earnings, 1900–1957", Review of Economics and Statistics. Vol. 45, pp. 374–385.

Keynes, J.M. (1930). *Essays in Persuasion*. New York: WW Norton, pp. 358–373.

Kochan, T. (2016). *Shaping the Future of Work*. New York: Business Expert Press.

Lebergott, S. (1964). *Manpower in Economic Growth*. New York: McGraw-Hill.

Rodgers, D. (2014). *The Work Ethic in Industrial America 1850–1920*, second edition. Chicago, IL: University of Chicago Press.

Ronen, S. and S. Primps (1981). "The Compressed Work Week as Organizational Change: Behavioral and Attitudinal Outcomes", *Academy of Management Review*. Vol. 6. pp. 61–74.

TINYpulse (2017). *The Broken Bridges of the Workplace: 2017 Employee Engagement Report*. www.tinypulse.com/hubfs/whitepaper/TINYpulse-2017-Employee-Engagement-Report-Broken-Bridges-of-the-workplace.pdf?t=1487009837061.

Weeks, J.D. (1883). US Department of the Interior Census Office, 1880 Census, Vol. 20: Report on the Statistics of Wages in the Manufacturing Industries with Supplementary Reports on the Average Retail Prices of the Necessaries of Life and on Trade Societies and Strikes and Lockouts. Washington, DC: US Department of the Interior Census Office.

Whaples, R. (2001). "Hours of Work in U.S. History", *Economic History Encyclopedia*. http://eh.net/encyclopedia/hours-of-work-in-u-s-history/.

Whaples, R. (1990). "Winning the Eight-Hour Day, 1909–1919", *The Journal of Economic History*. Vol. 50, pp. 393–406.

Wheatley, D. (2016). "Employee Satisfaction and Use of Flexible Working Arrangements", *Work, Employment and Society*. Vol. 31, pp. 1–19.

Zeisel, J. (1958). "The Workweek in American Industry 1850–1956", *Monthly Labor Review*. Vol. 81, pp. 23–29.

Nine

INTRODUCTION

Quite a few authors have speculated about the "future of work" in recent years, drawing conclusions that range from the idea that everyone will become an independent contractor rather than an employee to the idea that machines will do most of the work and people will just deal with a small number of activities such as providing personalized services and programming machines.

If anything can be learned from our experience in the computer age and the Internet age, it is that change in work does not happen as rapidly as predicted – but it does eventually arrive.

Today, most people work in services, not in manufacturing. Most people use computers for a significant part of their work and most people use the Internet for a significant part of their communications. Still, most people do work for organizations rather than as independent contractors, so that part of the picture has not changed so dramatically – though we are moving in that direction with contracting arrangements such as Uber and Airbnb, and even with products and services sold through Amazon and eBay.

Before getting further into the realm of ideas, perhaps it would be useful to review the state of work in the US today in terms of people's employment. Table 9.1 shows several categories of work that can be used to group American workers in the early 21st century.

It is clear from the Table 9.1 that most US working people are employed full-time, though 17% of the total workforce being in part-time employment is not trivial. Based on people's stated reasons for part-time work (not shown in Table 9.1), it appears that most people in such situations have chosen to work part-time for reasons other than not being able to find full-time work. In other words, only about 3.9% of the workforce is in part-time employment due to inability to find full-time work. This percentage has been fairly stable over time at between 2% and 4% of the labor force.

Table 9.1 Categories of Work

Arrangement	Number (and % of US Labor Force), 1950		Number (and % of US Labor Force), 1975		Number (and % of US Labor Force), 2000		Number (and % of US Labor Force), 2016	
Total US labor force	**64,599,000**	**100.0%**	**94,800,000**	**100.0%**	**141,489,000**	**100.0%**	**159,640,000**	**100.0%**
Working full-time for an employer	47,710,000	73.9%	78,454,000	82.8%	125,832,000	88.9%	142,243,000	89.1%
Working full-time, self-employed	10,505,000	16.3%	7,423,000	7.8%	9,798,000	6.9%	9,848,000	6.2%
Working part-time	10,174,000	15.7%	14,156,000	14.9%	25,087,000	17.7%	26,896,000	16.8%
Working more than one job	3,653,000 (1956)	5.7%	3,918,000	4.1%	7,70,000	5.7%	7,675,000	5.1%
Working in services sector	28,264,000	43.8%	55,758,000	58.8%	106,839,000	75.5%	120,641,000	75.6%
Working in manufacturing	16,166,000	25.0%	18,850,000	19.9%	18,301,000	12.9%	12,277,000	6.8%
Working in agriculture	7,497,000	11.6%	3,476,000	3.7%	2,232,0%	1.6%	2,180,0%	1.2%
Working in mining	936,000	1.5%	765,000	0.8%	538,000	0.4%	638,000	0.5%
Working in construction	2,454,000	3.8%	3,497,000	3.7%	6,725,000	4.8%	6,604,000	3.4%

Source: US Department of Labor, Bureau of Labor Statistics.

Sectoral employment has moved largely to services over time; the full set of services includes about 12% more of total employment, such that the sectors add to approximately 100%.

The number of people working for themselves is fairly low, at just 6.2% of the labor force. This percentage has been *declining* significantly over the past 50 years, from more than 16% of people in 1950. This is quite a striking trend, since at the same time the news today talks about the tendency for more people to work under non-permanent contracts (such as consulting arrangements) and about the "gig economy".[1]

As the long-term trend shows, it is clear that the self-employment phenomenon is limited. This is most likely due to three or four key elements. First, farming was a much greater part of the economy in 1950, employing about 12% of the workforce, with many farmers being self-employed. Farm employment has dropped to about 1% of total US employment today. Second, there is the fact that consultants and many sole practitioners have to generate their own business, so they are effectively entrepreneurs – which is not a lifestyle chosen by the majority of people. Third, many occupations such as doctors and dentists have moved from sole practitioners to joint practices linked to hospitals due to the costs of equipment and specialization of knowledge. Fourth, for all of these self-employment categories, contracting also brings the challenge of obtaining affordable health care benefits and retirement plans when working on such contracts versus having an employer who contributes to these costs. These are powerful forces toward organizational employment rather than individual employment.

With the growth of networks of companies and workers providing specific services in the value chain, we may expect to see the number of independent contractors increase. However, the growth has been quite limited thus far, and the challenges noted above make it unlikely that this independent work will grow very rapidly in the near future.

According to a study by Katz and Krueger (2016), the total amount of non-traditional work arrangements in use in the US in recent years covers more than 10% of the workforce. They found in a 2015 survey that "The percentage of workers engaged in alternative work arrangements – defined as temporary help agency workers, on-call workers, contract workers, and independent contractors or freelancers – rose from 10.7 percent in February 2005 to 15.8 percent in late 2015" (p. 1). They also found that people working for sharing services (or the "gig economy") such as Uber and Task Rabbit constituted just 0.5% of the workforce. This overall percentage is more than twice the size of the self-employed category presented by the US Department of Labor, primarily because the Katz and Krueger measure adds more categories of the workforce to obtain their "alternative work" measure.

HOW DOES THIS RELATE TO THE FOUR-DAY, 32-HOUR WORKWEEK?

A number of lessons can be drawn from these US data on jobs in recent years. First and foremost, the vast majority of jobs are in services sectors, and this reality will continue in the decades ahead. The US will not return to an agricultural or a primarily manufacturing-based economy. This is despite the fact that agricultural production has not disappeared and that domestic manufacturing still produces a much greater proportion of domestically consumed products than the percentage of jobs in that sector would imply. Both agriculture (Rasmussen 1982) and manufacturing (Gunn 1982; Muro 2017) have become highly mechanized in the US, so that total production does not reflect the proportion of jobs that one might otherwise expect. And both agricultural as well as manufacturing outputs in the US have grown over the years, despite declining employment in these sectors.

The graph in Figure 9.1 shows a number of interesting changes in US economic activity across major sectors in the past 60 years. For example, agriculture declined from 8.2% of the overall economic output in 1947 to just 1.1% in 2012. And manufacturing likewise declined from 25.8% of the economy to just 11.9%. The largest growth has been in financial services and other professional services, which went from 14% of the economy in 1947 to 32.6% in 2012. Education, health care and social services boomed from 1.5% of GDP in 1947 to 8.6% in 2012. And overall, services went from 55.3% of the economy to 77.0% of the total (or about 87% if you include construction, recreation, and some other services not listed).

So, given that almost 90% of jobs are in services today, how do trends toward somewhat greater independent contracting and somewhat greater movement to shorter-term employment relate to our theme of a four-day workweek? In fact, there are only slight implications for the 32-hour workweek. As long as companies (and governments) move to a four-day workweek, then the independent contractors and people in short-term employment will be able to follow the same conditions. This is unless they choose to work overtime, as could a person in a company with a longer-term employment contract.

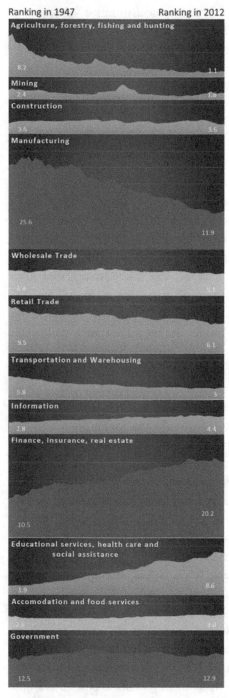

Ranking in 1947   Ranking in 2012

6622

Agriculture, forestry, fishing and hunting
8.2   1.1

Mining
2.4   1.8

Construction
3.6   3.6

Manufacturing
25.6   11.9

Wholesale Trade
6.4   5.7

Retail Trade
9.5   6.1

Transportation and Warehousing
5.8   3

Information
2.8   4.4

Finance, insurance, real estate
20.2   10.5

Educational services, health care and social assistance
1.9   8.6

Accomodation and food services
2.6   3.0

Government
12.5   12.9

Figure 9.1 Sectoral Percentages of US GDP

Source: US Bureau of Labor Statistics.

There may be implications of greater mechanization of work, as discussed in Chapter 6 above, but these implications are not affected by the potential growth of independent contracting.

PART-TIME VS. FULL-TIME WORKERS

The use of part-time workers has been both a boon and a bane to US employment over the past 50 years. Part-time workers allow companies to fill in work needs without adding head count to their payrolls, and part-time work allows people with other commitments (e.g., mothers with babies, students in school) to pursue both activities. At the same time, part-time work places people in a weak position with respect to non-salary benefits such as pensions and health care, since most organizations limit these benefits to full-time workers. The cost to a company in terms of compensation is lower for two half-time workers than for one full-time worker[2] – plus there are no labor rules governing the company's right to lay off part-time workers.

This presents a curious challenge to the individual as well as to the company. If an individual wants assured access to a company's health and retirement benefits, then he/she will have to work at least 20 hours per week. If a company wants to offer the 32-hour workweek, then there is no inherent conflict with having full-time employees, though it reduces the difference between part-time and full-time employees. Even for people working part-time above the maximum limit, between 20 and 40 hours per week, there is a perceived bias in employment opportunities within a company, because people working the "full" workweek of 40 hours are seen as being first in line for promotions and wage/salary increases. Those working fewer hours are seen as less-committed to the company and/or less central to the company's needs.[3] With a 32-hour workweek, more people would be able to take advantage of the full workweek and the perception of being employed full-time.

The part-time versus full-time label is thus complicated by both the legal issue of fringe benefits associated with full-time status of an employee and the perception issue of people working less than the full workweek being seen as either less valuable or less committed. It is also complicated with company concerns about having flexibility in the workforce, such that if demand for its products or services declines (or increases) even temporarily, the company wants to be able to adjust its workforce downward (or upward) without significant constraints.

Temporary or part-time workers fill this need nicely, but then they suffer the fragility of their employment being subject to market conditions that are beyond their ability to influence. These various considerations make it unlikely that the US workforce will move toward much greater reliance on part-time work, at least in the near-term future.

FLEXIBLE SCHEDULES

Considering just full-time workers, there is a movement underway to make the workday more flexible in terms of the specific hours worked and the location of the work. This is not relevant in the cases of jobs such as working at a restaurant, hotel, hospital, school, or other activity where physical interaction with customers/clients is required. Even in these cases, however, there are activities that can be structured to be carried out on a different timetable or in a different location, such as record-keeping, dealing with suppliers, human resource management, and others. And in many businesses, such as banking and other financial services, but also education and health services, some of the services can be provided at a distance through electronic means (e.g., the Internet). ATMs are a well-known example of electronic delivery of financial services, but even in this case, a "smart" ATM can connect to a person in a call center-type location where additional financial services can be rendered via the mechanism of the ATM.[4] Distance education through the Internet has already become quite popular, and many training programs as well as some university courses are available through this channel. Medical services offered with the assistance of doctors and nurses providing guidance at a distance through the Internet are also becoming more common.[5] In all of these instances, services can be provided on a 24/7 basis, and work hours can be assigned flexibly to teams of people at the provider.

The main positive aspects of flexible work hours include:

1. The ability for employees to deal with non-work responsibilities such as childcare, education, and health care.
2. Potentially reduced commuting times if people can arrive at work at non-traditional times of day.
3. Likely improvement in job satisfaction as people feel they have more control over their time.

4. Companies should experience greater productivity if employees are more satisfied.
5. More use of electronic means of communicating such as e-mail, phone and videoconferencing may enable companies to thrive in the digital age, where virtual teams are often very useful.

The main negative aspects of flexible work hours include:

1. Difficulty in scheduling face-to-face meetings when all employees are not in the workplace at the same time.
2. Feeling by employees that they are somewhat out of touch with corporate activities and interactions with co-workers and bosses, which could reduce recognition of their performance and limit advancement.
3. Difficulty for companies to evaluate performance and slacking behavior when people are not visible.

Evaluations of flexible work arrangements show fairly varied responses. A recent Gallup poll of about 10,000 Americans showed that the most satisfied among them were people working part of the time at home and part of the time at the office.[6]

In a meta-analysis of several dozen studies of flexible work arrangements, Baltes (1999) found that flexible work schedules positively influenced a number of performance and satisfaction measures, including productivity, job satisfaction, and reduced absenteeism. At the same time, Baltes found that flexible hours did not have a significant impact on managerial and professional employees. This will remain a challenge for alternative work arrangements in the future, since these professionals often cannot structure their work more flexibly – though perhaps it is already fairly flexible before the new arrangement.[7]

Overall, there is quite a bit of opportunity today to structure the workweek more flexibly than in the past, given the availability of technology that allows people to work from various locations and to communicate fluidly via telephone, e-mail, teleconferencing, and other electronic means. Flexibility does not mean banishing some people to work from home or otherwise at a distance, but rather it means giving people the opportunity to use that alternative from time to time as is helpful to their individual circumstances.

CONTRACTEES VS. EMPLOYEES

As work becomes increasingly mechanized and as companies outsource more activities in the value-added chain, the use of contract employees is increasing. As was noted at the beginning of this chapter, the amount of contracting at present is small, though it is probably under-measured because contract workers may appear as self-employed and/or as people who have full-time jobs but who also moonlight as contractees.

The major costs to the individual of working as a contractee are: (1) that he/she has no health or pension benefits associated with the work; and (2) the work itself is not usually assured on an ongoing basis (i.e., there is no job security). These are real challenges, and ones that must be faced if this arrangement is to grow in the future. Malone (2004), as discussed below, has suggestions for dealing with these two costs.

FASTER JOB ROTATION

Baby boomers certainly scratch their heads at the job-hopping done by many if not most millennials.[8] While baby boomers did not face the same job-for-life prospects as their parents or grandparents, they still have demonstrated a fairly long-term duration of working for a single employer. According to the US Bureau of Labor Statistics, in 2016, "the median tenure of workers ages 55 to 64 (10.1 years) was more than three times that of workers ages 25 to 34 years (2.8 years)."[9] The full distribution for selected years since 1983 appears in Table 9.2.

So much for the notion of job-hopping millennials! The earlier baby boomer and Gen X generations also demonstrated the same propensity to shift jobs during their 20s and early 30s, while becoming much more stable in their employment after age 55. From 1983 to 2016, the average number of years with their current employer for people over age 25 went from 5.0 years to 5.1 years. And for those in their 20s and 30s, the average number of years with the current employer went from 3.0 years in 1983 to 2.8 years in 2016 – not much of a change. Of course, we can always say that "this time is different" when referring to the post-Global Financial Crisis era, but the big changes that one might have expected during the computer age and the Internet age have not produced major shifts in job tenure by age category.

TECHNOLOGY CHANGE

As noted in detail in Chapter 8 above, technology change is a major factor in reshuffling the job panorama in the US and around the

Table 9.2 Median Years of Tenure with Current Employer for Employed
Wage and Salary Workers by Age and Sex, Selected Years, 1983–2016

Age and Sex	Jan. 1983	Jan. 2000	Jan. 2006	Jan. 2010	Jan. 2014	Jan. 2016
Total						
16 years and over	3.5	3.5	4.0	4.4	4.6	4.2
16–17 years	0.7	0.6	0.6	0.7	0.7	0.6
18–19 years	0.8	0.7	0.7	1.0	0.8	0.8
20–24 years	1.5	1.1	1.3	1.5	1.3	1.3
25 years and over	5.0	4.7	4.9	5.2	5.5	5.1
25–34 years	3.0	2.6	2.9	3.1	3.0	2.8
35–44 years	5.2	4.8	4.9	5.1	5.2	4.9
45–54 years	9.5	8.2	7.3	7.8	7.9	7.9
55–64 years	12.2	10.0	9.3	10.0	10.4	10.1
65 years and over	9.6	9.5	8.8	9.9	10.3	10.3
Men						
16 years and over	4.1	3.8	4.1	4.6	4.7	4.3
16–17 years	0.7	0.6	0.7	0.7	0.7	0.6
18–19 years	0.8	0.7	0.7	1.0	0.9	0.8
20–24 years	1.5	1.2	1.4	1.6	1.4	1.3
25 years and over	5.9	5.0	5.0	5.3	5.5	5.2
25–34 years	3.2	2.7	2.9	3.2	3.1	2.9
35–44 years	7.3	5.4	5.1	5.3	5.4	5.0
45–54 years	12.8	9.5	8.1	8.5	8.2	8.4
55–64 years	15.3	10.2	9.5	10.4	10.7	10.2
65 years and over	8.3	9.1	8.3	9.7	10.0	10.2
Women						
16 years and over	3.1	3.3	3.9	4.2	4.5	4.0
16–17 years	0.7	0.6	0.6	0.7	0.7	0.6
18–19 years	0.8	0.7	0.7	1.0	0.8	0.8
20–24 years	1.5	1.0	1.2	1.5	1.3	1.2
25 years and over	4.2	4.4	4.8	5.1	5.4	5.0
25–34 years	2.8	2.5	2.8	3.0	2.9	2.6
35–44 years	4.1	4.3	4.6	4.9	5.1	4.8
45–54 years	6.3	7.3	6.7	7.1	7.6	7.5
55–64 years	9.8	9.9	9.2	9.7	10.2	10.0
65 years and over	10.1	9.7	9.5	10.1	10.5	10.4

Source: Bureau of Labor Statistics, www.bls.gov/news.release/pdf/tenure.pdf.

world. This may not mean more frequent changes of employer, but it does mean changes of employment activity. Mechanized agriculture has changed the face of farming in all but the most isolated and intractable communities in all countries and has resulted in far fewer farmers than in previous generations. Today's farmers have to be able to operate more sophisticated machines and to deal with information about markets and supplies that come from electronic sources, typically through the Internet. Likewise, in manufacturing, at least in the Triad countries, mechanization has reduced the number of workers per production site significantly, so that people are moving to other types of employment. In manufacturing businesses, the jobs have migrated from the production line to promotion, purchasing, management of the supply chain, and other ancillary but important activities. Even with these adjustments in agriculture and manufacturing, the services sectors are growing and absorbing the bulk of employees.

In services sectors as well, technology is changing the production of the services and the job activities of employees. Jobs that used to require limited skills, such as bank tellers or secretaries, are being replaced by more complex jobs, such as bank customer service representatives and office assistants. Jobs that have been replaced by machines, such as a lot of record-keeping functions, have been replaced by jobs that evaluate the records and interact with the machines, jobs to maintain the machines, and even jobs to program and redesign the machines. The direction of change is away from routine tasks toward more sophisticated tasks and toward tasks that involve interaction with clients/customers.

ECONOMIC COST CHANGES (ESPECIALLY IN COMMUNICATIONS AND TRANSPORTATION)

Certainly, one of the central reasons for job adjustments in the past half-century has been the reduction of costs in communications[10] and in transportation. Through the Internet, the cost of telecommunications has fallen close to zero, with instant communication available around the world even with videoconference capability. As a result of greater efficiencies in shipping (e.g., through the use of standardized 20-foot and 40-foot containers) and lower regulatory costs due to lower tariffs around the world, transportation of goods is also much less costly than it was half a century ago. Figures 9.2 and 9.3 show the persistent trend toward lower transport costs for air and ocean shipping over the past 40 years.

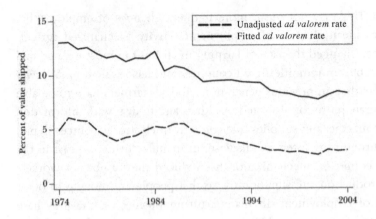

Figure 9.2 Air Transport Costs since 1974

Note: The unadjusted *ad valorem* rate is simply expenditure/import value. The fitted *ad valorem* rate is derived from a regression and controls for changes in the mix of trade partners and products traded.

Source: Hummels (2007). Author's calculation based on US Census Bureau's *U.S. Imports of Merchandise*.

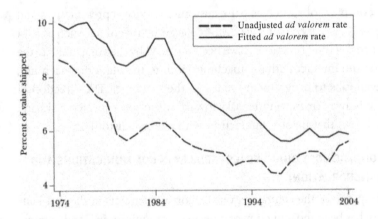

Figure 9.3 Ocean Transport Costs since 1974

Note: The unadjusted *ad valorem* rate is simply expenditure/import value. The fitted *ad valorem* rate is derived from a regression and controls for changes in the mix of trade partners and products traded.

Source: Hummels (2007). Author's calculation based on US Census Bureau's *U.S. Imports of Merchandise*.

NEW WORK MODELS – UBER, ACE HARDWARE, AIRBNB, AND EBAY

Consider just four cases of 21st century companies that shook the foundations of "traditional" business in the US established during the 20th century: Uber, the car service that parallels taxi service with independent drivers operating their own vehicles and contracting with Uber as drivers just as customers contract with Uber as passengers; Ace Hardware, a consortium of independent hardware store owners who operate under a single brand name and who use centralized purchasing and transport to lower their operating costs; Airbnb, the room rental service that competes with traditional hotels to provide visitors with accommodations for short-term stays via the platform that unites providers of rooms with guests; and eBay, the e-commerce website that connects vendors and customers through its website, allowing an enormous range of suppliers to present their wares to potential customers, who in turn make their purchases through the eBay website. [11]

Uber and its primary competitor, Lyft, provide effectively a taxi service through a network of independent vehicle owners and customers who are connected through the computer system operated by Uber (or Lyft). These companies enable vehicle owners to "share" their vehicles with strangers in exchange for compensation according to a calculation structure set up by Uber to cover operating costs plus a profit/income for the ride provider and a revenue for Uber. In metropolitan areas, where there are enough riders and drivers available, the service operates quite fluidly. When drivers (providers of rides) are fewer, it is more difficult to run the driver–rider connection service. Nevertheless, by 2017, Uber was operating in 570 cities around the world. It was founded in 2009.

Ace Hardware, a brand name that is well known in the US and in many other countries, is actually a consortium of independent hardware stores rather than a single company. The organization was formed in 1924 by several Chicago-area hardware store owners to pool their efforts to purchase inventory and to have a visible brand name. Ace has grown to a network of 4,700 stores in dozens of countries. The organization has established about 100 group-owned hardware stores in addition to the 4,600 independent ones today. So, Ace is effectively a purchasing consortium that also provides a common brand name and typically a common store style. While this example is not new in the 21st century, the business model is non-traditional and reflects the network-style collaborations between companies and customers. In principle, all shopping can be done through the Ace website, with hardware items shipped from supplier to customer and arranged by Ace. However, the group prefers to channel customers when possible to local Ace Hardware member stores, so pricing reflects that bias.

Airbnb is a marketplace for hotel-like accommodations literally around the world. It was founded in 2008. The company connects people who choose to make sleeping rooms available for short-term rental with customers who seek non-hotel lodging alternatives. In this instance, the issue of trust is hugely important. Potential customers want to ensure that the accommodations are in good condition and that the services offered are really available. Potential room renters want to make sure that their clients are not destructive or otherwise undesirable as users of the service. As a result, Airbnb spends inordinate amounts of time and money making the effort to ensure that each experience is as advertised and that the customers are good citizens as well. With 3 million listings worldwide and over 160 million guests served so far, Airbnb seems to have found a formula that works.

eBay is an e-commerce web-based company that allows thousands of individuals and companies to present their products and services on its website and then enables potential customers to both explore the products and services virtually and to make purchases when they want. eBay operates free to buyers, while sellers pay a fee to list and a fee when sales occur. The company was founded in 1995 as an online auction site connecting consumers and vendors of products and services. It has expanded to include a general-purpose web store through which people can buy and sell directly or through the auction format.

All four of these examples demonstrate the "new" kind of business that allows small or large companies and even individuals to sell their products and services through a central website. Delivery of the service or product may be at the customer's home or office or at a location offered by the seller (e.g., an Airbnb room or an Ace Hardware store). These structures enable a world of business in which markets are effectively global and consumers/customers are able to shop without dealing with big stores or big companies – and vendors can find customers without themselves being large or financially well endowed.

MALONE'S NETWORKS IDEA

Thomas Malone (2004) described a new organizational order that is coming to replace the hierarchies of traditional large companies. His view

Centralized	←			→ Decentralized

Type of decision-making	Centralized hierarchy	Loose hierarchy	Democracy	Market
Examples	Military organization; political kingdom	Consulting firm; research university; European Union	Political democracy; medical clinic; Unitarian church	Free market; the internet; internal market in a company

Figure 9.4 The Decentralization Continuum

Source: Adapted from Malone (2004, p. 6).

is that more decentralized decision-making is possible today, and this enables people to work in a variety of new ways that allow them more freedom and more control over their own lives. He paints a picture of historical development from original societies that were hunter–gathers, with no hierarchy, to agrarian societies with strong hierarchies, to looser hierarchies in the last century with mechanized production and central governments that offered military protection to citizens. He argues that today government is again becoming more localized, as national security becomes less of a challenge and technology permits decentralization. He asserts that, with the Internet and with low transportation costs for goods, we are at a point where highly decentralized decision-making is possible once again in both business and government contexts.

Malone's continuum (Figure 9.4) shows that there is a place for each type of decision-making structure, but that the centralized hierarchy is useful today only in the context of military organizations and perhaps political kingdoms. The more appropriate organizational structure for business activities is the market-based structure in which people become largely independent contractors, selling their labor services in networks that bring together providers of needed services and then making resulting products and services available through outlets such as Amazon.com or eBay. This future does not imply a lack of government, since someone still needs to define and enforce the rules of the game. But even in government, much of the decision-making can be pushed to local levels where people can make clear decisions about use of their tax dollars and services that they want to have provided by the government sector.

THE DIGITAL AGE OF SCHMIDT AND COHEN

Eric Schmidt (co-founder of Google) and Jared Cohen (2013) discuss the implications of the Internet becoming the central technology of the present and the medium-term future. They argue that the transformation of society due to the Internet, from online marketplaces to health care provided at great distance to learning from teachers and contents around the globe, is just in its initial stage, and that much more change is yet to come from this innovation.

They look at the implications of having a virtual world that coexists with the real world and both enhances it as well as partially replaces it. For example, what is the need for stores if a consumer can order any product online, and even experience it to some extent through virtual reality? The replacement of stores by Amazon.com and other online vendors is indicative that this may very well mark a major shift in buying behavior now and in the future.

And what is the meaning of an emerging market if people everywhere can gain access to the same teaching from the best teachers and products from the most efficient and innovative producers? The governments of the world will struggle to catch up with this new reality, but they will not be able to stop it.[12] Emerging markets will not disappear, and income inequality will remain a major challenge, but people's access to information will permeate even the lowest-income locations around the world.

Schmidt and Cohen (2013) explore the world of the future in this Internet-driven or Internet-enabled environment. But their perspective does not detract from the idea of the four-day workweek because, like Malone (2004), they are looking at greater decentralization of decision-making rather than at the replacement of work with something else. Perhaps implicit in their view is that less time will be needed for work in the future, and thus the conditions will be even more favorable for a four-day workweek.

JACOB MORGAN'S FUTURE OF WORK FOR EMPLOYEES AND EMPLOYERS

Jacob Morgan (2014) argues that the future will largely contain people who are either self-employed (e.g., as contractors) or who work for organizations that allow them great flexibility as to when and where to do their work. This is not greatly different from Malone's (2004) perspective that focuses on decentralization of business activity as well. Morgan (2014) is more prescriptive, arguing that companies will need to offer more flexible schedules and locations to their employees – or lose employees to the organizations that will. As for employees, Morgan reasons that they need to be much more flexible in their own willingness to work on different tasks and to adapt themselves to a changing environment.

He notes that an element of work that strongly supports the flexibility approach is commuting. Why should people spend half an hour each way, or often much more than that, driving or taking public transportation to work when they could accomplish much more using that time to either do the work itself or use the time for something else that would motivate their work even more? Commuting less frequently or at off-hours would deal with this obstacle and presumably lead to greater enjoyment of work. Morgan expects that this will be part of the pressure that produces a "freelancer economy" in which people sell their work to companies on a contractual basis and decide how much time and when they want to work. This outcome may be a bit far-fetched for most people today, but technology and job opportunities are indeed pushing in this direction. These changes and those noted in the previous two examples of futurist thinking do nothing to hinder the four-day workweek; in fact, Morgan's kind of flexibility would be even better served when people work for four days instead of five each week.

WHAT DO PEOPLE WANT FROM A JOB? INCOME, FRIENDS, SAFETY, HEALTH, ROUTINE, FREEDOM/FLEXIBILITY, CREATIVITY, FREEDOM IN DECISION-MAKING, AND HIERARCHY VS. DEMOCRACY

The future of work necessarily relates to what people want from a job – and what a job can offer them. If someone wants a job that offers permanent stability and future income, this is probably not feasible today or ever in history, as technology, politics, and economics change. If someone wants an income and reasonable hope for security in the future, then jobs that are less subject to mechanization or to outsourcing are good choices – except that it is devilishly difficult to say which jobs won't be subject to these kinds of pressure in the future. While permanent stability may not be possible, certainly medium-term stability (say, for five years) is a reasonable target, and many jobs do offer that kind of profile. For example, professionals such as doctors, lawyers, engineers, and scientists, once they find "permanent" positions, are likely to have such medium-term stability. And likewise people working in personal services such as haircutters, house cleaners, lawn mowers, plumbers, handymen, and many others are not likely to be replaced by machines or outsourced to China.

This subject was discussed in Chapter 2, and the idea is not to restate the same points, but rather to emphasize that work in the future will continue to offer these outcomes and that people will continue to desire both income and other features of work. When we move to a four-day, 32-hour workweek, there will be no new goals of work, but there will be more time to choose among alternatives, from more work to more sleep and many things in between.

CONCLUSIONS

The nature of work is definitely changing, but from the historical perspective covering the past 200 years, this is not new. Maybe the pace of change is more rapid today, but a shifting employment landscape is the rule rather than the exception over time. Several examples of contemporary organizations (eBay, Uber, Ace Hardware and Airbnb) show that an Internet-based business model is becoming more and more common and permitting more and more decentralization of decision-making for both buyers and sellers of goods and services. This does not mean the end of retail stores or big companies, but it does support the ideas of all of the futurist authors discussed above who talked about the need for greater flexibility in jobs and in people.

The fact that costs of communication and transportation have dropped so dramatically over the past half-century really sets the stage for greater work flexibility. The ways in which people can take advantage of these lower costs range from taking more vacations to working from a distance via electronic means. It should not be ignored that, in the US today, about 90% of people work in services, where these technology advances are readily applicable. It would be a lot harder to work on a farm from a distance or to operate a manufacturing facility at a distance (other than hiring someone else to do it!).

The four-day workweek is coming, one way or another. It may arrive in fits and starts, with some companies allowing individuals to work a shorter workweek, and then the model taking off. It may be championed by one company or a small group of companies. And/or it may come as a spin-off of the greater flexibility in workweeks that allow people to work some of the time from home and on schedules that are more adjustable. Regardless, the elements are in place, and the outcome just remains to materialize.

Table A9.1 Employed Persons by Class of Worker and Part-Time Status (In Thousands)

Category	Not Seasonally Adjusted			Seasonally Adjusted					
	Dec. 2015	Nov. 2016	Dec. 2016	Dec. 2015	Aug. 2016	Sept. 2016	Oct. 2016	Nov. 2016	Dec. 2016
Class of worker									
Agriculture and related industries	2,273	2,366	2,180	2,455	2,505	2,429	2,317	2,431	2,356
Wage and salary workers[1]	1,482	1,535	1,366	1,594	1,597	1,522	1,493	1,559	1,470
Self-employed workers, unincorporated	760	796	797	819	874	890	817	833	857
Unpaid family workers	32	34	18	—	—	—	—	—	—
Nonagricultural industries	147,430	150,020	149,617	147,635	149,170	149,526	149,604	149,752	149,811
Wage and salary workers[1]	138,989	141,210	140,753	139,025	140,431	140,739	140,806	140,968	140,773
Government	20,905	21,114	21,029	20,755	20,701	20,809	20,968	20,938	20,865
Private industries	118,083	120,096	119,724	118,278	119,682	119,990	120,073	120,016	119,916
Private households	735	717	680	—	—	—	—	—	—
Other industries	117,348	119,380	119,044	117,511	118,932	119,241	119,325	119,290	119,206
Self-employed workers, unincorporated	8,386	8,757	8,800	8,576	8,631	8,599	8,731	8,716	8,991
Unpaid family workers	55	53	64	—	—	—	—	—	—
Person at work part-time[2]									
All industries									
Part-time for economic reasons[3]	6,179	5,518	5,707	6,057	6,027	5,874	5,850	5,659	5,598
Slack work or business conditions	3,678	3,391	3,478	3,589	3,736	3,587	3,481	3,485	3,401
Could only find part-time work	2,129	1,853	1,828	2,175	1,907	1,972	2,093	1,902	1,873
Part-time for non-economic reasons[4]	20,585	22,084	21,711	20,173	20,575	20,742	20,765	21,059	21,251

(continued)

Table A9.1 [Cont.]

Category	Not Seasonally Adjusted			Seasonally Adjusted					
	Dec. 2015	Nov. 2016	Dec. 2016	Dec. 2015	Aug. 2016	Sept. 2016	Oct. 2016	Nov. 2016	Dec. 2016
Nonagricultural industries									
Part-time for economic reasons[3]	6,046	5,411	5,561	5,948	5,903	5,770	5,748	5,550	5,476
Slack work or business conditions	3,594	3,327	3,362	3,531	3,599	3,510	3,415	3,424	3,310
Could only find part-time work	2,123	1,832	1,824	2,164	1,903	1,959	2,082	1,870	1,862
Part-time for non-economic reasons[4]	20,294	21,757	21,335	19,888	20,261	20,409	20,455	20,696	20,818

1 Includes self-employed workers whose businesses are incorporated.

2 Refers to those who worked 1–34 hours during the survey reference week and excludes employed persons who were absent from their jobs for the entire week.

3 Refers to those who worked 1–34 hours during the reference week for an economic reason such as slack work or unfavorable business conditions, inability to find full-time work, or seasonal declines in demand.

4 Refers to persons who usually work part-time for non-economic reasons such as childcare problems, family or personal obligations, school or training, retirement or Social Security limits on earnings, and other reasons. This excludes persons who usually work full-time but worked only 1–34 hours during the reference week for reasons such as vacations, holidays, illness, and bad weather.

–: Data not available.

Note: Detail for the seasonally adjusted data shown in this table will not necessarily add to totals because of the independent seasonal adjustment of the various series. Updated population controls are introduced annually with the release of January data.

Source: US Bureau of Labor Statistics, www.bls.gov/news.release/.

NOTES

1 Estimates of the number of people who work this way are quite varied, but always show a small percentage of the total work force. See, for example, www. bls.gov/careeroutlook/2016/article/what-is-the-gig-economy.htm. Some of the pros and cons are discussed in https://hbr.org/2016/10/who-wins-in-the-gig-economy-and-who-loses.

2 US law generally considers part-time work to be less than half-time, or 20 hours per week (less than 1000 hours per year). By keeping under this limit, employers are generally able to avoid offering employees participation in company health plans and company retirement plans. See, for example, http://work.chron.com/fulltime-benefits-vs-parttime-benefits-18972.html.

3 A study in 2009 in Australia (McDonald et al. 2009) showed that people working part-time faced reduced responsibilities and less access to high-status roles and projects, a lack of access to promotion opportunities, increased work intensity, and poor workplace support.

4 See, for example, www.atmmarketplace.com/articles/unlocking-the-potential-of-self-service-with-smart-atms/.

5 There is even a journal of Internet-based medical support, The Journal of Medical Internet Research (www.jmir.org/2001/2/e20/), which has been in existence for more than a decade.

6 See https://qz.com/908116/the-happiest-worker-spends-about-one-day-a-week-in-the-office/.

7 The challenge for flextime and compressed workweeks is that the managers cannot easily restructure their hours similar to the workers. With a four-day, 32-hour workweek, this would not present the same problem. Everyone would have the three-day weekend.

8 Baby boomers are generally defined as people born between 1945 and 1965. Millennials are defined as people born between 1980 and 2000. (And Generation X consists of people born between 1965 and 1980.)

9 BLS (2016). "Employee Tenure in 2016", News Release. September 26, 2016, www. bls.gov/news.release/pdf/tenure.pdf.

10 Malone (2004) argues that reductions in communication costs are the fundamental driver of the new organizational forms that are arising in the 21st century.

11 There is no intent here to disparage Amazon.com, the most valuable of the e-commerce ventures. Given our focus on the workweek, eBay is discussed as one of these types of business, and Amazon is widely discussed elsewhere (e.g., www. academia.edu/8744694/Amazon.com_Inc._a_case_study_analysis).

12 One could argue that it is possible to stop the Internet, as North Korea has done in that isolated country, or as China has done by disallowing access by Internet service providers from outside and websites that show information that the government does not want to allow people there to see.

REFERENCES

Baltes, B., T. Briggs, J. Huff, J. Wright, and G. Neuman (1999). "Flexible and Compressed Workweek Schedules: A Meta-Analysis of Their Effects on Work-Related Criteria". *Journal of Applied Psychology*. Vol. 84, pp. 496–513.

Gunn, T. (1982). "The Mechanization of Design and Manufacturing", *Scientific American*. Vol. 247, pp. 114–130.

Hummels, D. (2007). "Transportation Costs and International Trade in the Second Era of Globalization", *Journal of Economic Perspectives*. Vol. 21, pp. 131–154.

Katz, L. and A. Krueger (2016). "The Rise and Nature of Alternative Work Arrangements in the United States, 1995–2015", NBER *Working Paper No. 22667*. Cambridge, MA: NBER.

Malone, T. (2004). *The Future of Work: How the New Order of Business Will Shape Your Organization, Your Management Style and Your Life.* Cambridge, MA: Harvard Business Review Press.

McDonald, P., L. Bradley, and K. Brown (2009). "'Full-time is a Given Here': Part-time versus Full-time Job Quality", *British Journal of Management*. Vol. 20, pp. 143–157.

Morgan, J. (2014). *The Future of Work*. New York: Wiley.

Muro, M. (2017). "Manufacturing Jobs Aren't Coming Back", MIT *Technology Review*, www.technologyreview.com/s/602869/manufacturing-jobs-arent-coming-back/.

Rasmussen, W. (1982). "The Mechanization of Agriculture", *Scientific American*. Vol. 247, pp. 77–89.

Schmidt, E. and J. Cohen (2013). *The New Digital Age*. New York: Vintage Books.

Thompson, D. (2012). "Where Did All the Workers Go?", *The Atlantic*, .

Ten

INTRODUCTION

From the very beginning of this project, I have heard frequent if not constant assertions that "this won't work." While the evidence and reasoning laid out in previous chapters would hopefully be sufficient to respond to this knee-jerk reaction about the four-day workweek, it is probably useful to work through some specifics of the negative perspective.

Specific reasons why the four-day workweek might not work include the most important single one: people won't change from their current habits and mind-set that a five-day workweek is normal and appropriate and that 40 hours of work per week (or more for non-hourly people) is fine. Subsets of that logic include the argument that people won't accept a (slight) reduction in income in order to have an extra day free each week, and that companies will not be able to sustain the cost of losing work hours without a corresponding equal reduction in pay to workers. Another obstacle that is perceived by some people is that eliminating production (particularly of services) on Fridays will cause an insurmountable cost to society when those services are no longer available on that day.

These and several other contentions about the problems of moving to a four-day, 32-hour workweek are confronted and to a large extent refuted in the pages below. At the end of the day, there is no question that costs will be incurred during the transition period of perhaps four to five years as the four-day week is introduced in companies, government agencies, and other organizations. However, those costs will be manageable and will be overcome, leaving a much-improved workweek in operation afterward.

REASONS WHY IT WON'T WORK

Cost to the Workers in Lost Income and Companies in Lost Output

Of course this is a huge issue, since people count on their existing incomes and would be shocked by a decline in salary or wages. The challenge is to see who, in fact, would prefer a somewhat reduced income in order to have an extra weekend day to use for other activities. The four-day workweek would not force everyone to drop to 32 hours of work each week instead of 40. The four-day workweek would *allow* people to choose that alternative. Anyone wishing to remain on the 40-hour workweek would simply be paid overtime (at the existing rate of compensation) for the extra eight hours. The cost and benefits of this shift, along with the expected changes in productivity that would likely accompany the shift, were explored in Chapter 5 in some detail. A bit of that content is restated here to reinforce the key points that: (1) the move to the 32-hour workweek is voluntary; and (2) as a result of productivity increases and distribution of the costs of the adjustment over time, the impact on workers will not be a major 20% reduction in income, but rather far less.

Workers Pay the Cost of Reduced Hours or Work

If we assume for the moment that companies do not pay any of the cost of reduced work hours, then workers will incur the full cost. If workers are compensated according to their productivity, then other things being equal, they would receive income increases of about 2% per year, recouping their original income levels in about nine years. If productivity only grows at the last decade's rate of about 1.5% per year, then it would take about 12 years to recoup the original income level. This is a substantial hit to near-term earnings, and many people likely would choose to work some overtime hours beyond 32 per week to keep their incomes closer to the original level and growth rate.

However, it is likely that the initial reduction in work hours will produce a jump in productivity, as workers become more motivated by the reduced workweek. This certainly was the case with Ford Motor Company in 1926, and also in other more limited experiments with reduced workweeks elsewhere. If the initial move to the 32-hour workweek produced a one-time productivity bump of, say, 8–10%, then this would allow companies to adjust wages/salaries much quicker, leading to a perhaps three- to four-year time period for recouping workers' original incomes and growth paths.

While we cannot know exactly how much of a jump in productivity will accompany the four-day workweek, companies could impose rules such as perhaps a 10% initial wage reduction in exchange for the 20% reduction in work hours per week, and then review productivity results after the first year to see if the subsequent trajectory of incomes can be restored or if further adjustment might be needed. Obviously, this is speculative, and contracts would need to incorporate contingencies for what turn out to be the actual productivity gains. This method still places all of the burden on the employees.

Companies Pay the Cost of Reduced Hours of Work

Companies could agree to shoulder the entire adjustment cost, as Ford Motor Company did when moving from the 48-hour workweek to the 40-hour workweek in 1926, with no wage or salary reductions. Apparently, the productivity improvement at that time was commensurate with the wages being paid, so that Ford did not suffer a huge corporate income drop in the year after the policy was implemented. If companies choose to take this position of not reducing weekly salaries/wages, then they run the risk of encountering *ex post* smaller productivity increases and therefore reduced profits in the short term. This would probably not be attractive to publicly traded companies, but it would not preclude other kinds of organizations from pursuing the 32-hour workweek and keeping wages/salaries the same.[1]

Companies and Workers Share Costs of the Reduced Workweek

A third way to approach the cost of cutting work hours by 20% per week is to share that cost between employees and employers. If the employees agree to a 10% compensation cut while employers agree to absorb whatever lower production (and thus cost) the reduced work hours create, then the burden would be shared. This author expects, across industries as an average, about a 10% improvement in productivity from employees in the first year of operation of the four-day workweek due to their greater satisfaction and motivation from the shorter workweek. If this occurs, companies will suffer no loss and workers will have to recoup their earnings over subsequent years. Maybe the burden should be a 5% cut in salaries/wages, with companies bearing the rest of the expected cost, which (according to my estimate of a 10% productivity improvement) would also be 5%. Many possibilities exist for this burden-sharing. A key point is that the burden is expected to be much smaller than the reduction in work hours, assuming that productivity does indeed jump due to the greater employee motivation/satisfaction under the new rules.

So, with the various alternatives for sharing the cost of adjustment to a four-day, 32-hour workweek, we can see that there is plenty of room for creative solutions. It seems plausible to share the expected costs between employers and employees, but this may not be acceptable in all organizations. And the risk of productivity increases being greater or smaller than an anticipated value means that some arrangement is needed to manage that risk. Most likely the way to approach this challenge would be to find some companies that are willing to pursue the four-day workweek and then show through demonstration that it works (and that unexpected complications can be dealt with).

The adjustment can also be aided by government policy intervention to subsidize companies that introduce the four-day workweek and to support employees who move to this model. The policy could be as simple as a tax credit or deduction for the costs that companies incur to maintain their production levels or a tax rate reduction for the lower incomes incurred by workers.[2]

It Has Always Been Thus

Social psychology and behavioral economics teach us that people get ideas fixed in their minds, and then it is very difficult to budge them from these ideas. The communists are the enemy. Women cannot do science. Africans are lazy. People from New York are in too much of a hurry. All of these generalizations have popped up in recent history, and all of them have been shown to be incorrect. However, once people get any of these ideas or others fixed in their minds, it is difficult to displace them. Tversky and Kahnemann (1974) described this behavior as "anchoring," in which people observe/experience some phenomenon or information and then use it to form judgments for future decisions or interpretations. For example, if US house prices increased by an average of about 10% per year during 1994–2004, which they did, then this must be the permanent outlook for house prices, which it was not, as the Global Financial Crisis demonstrated.

Based on this kind of reasoning, the workweek must be 40 hours over five days, because "it has always been thus" – never mind that it has not always been thus, and that subtle and not-so-subtle changes have occurred ever since that paradigm was established in 1926. Breaking this paradigm will not be easy. Organized labor has long ago switched from pursuing shorter work hours to pursuing greater job security and worker benefits such as health and retirement programs. Organized labor itself has been in continuing decline since the 1950s, so maybe that is not a good point of reference today. People are much more concerned today about being replaced by machines or by Chinese production than they are worried about how many days off they have each week.[3] Figure 10.1 shows results of a survey for the World Economic Forum of people in 25 countries in 2016 on the subject of their most significant worries. The results point to job loss as the single most important item, followed by corruption, poverty and inequality, crime and violence, and health care.

Given these results, it appears that people are much less concerned about the number of hours that they work and much more concerned about having a job at all. This is perhaps not surprising after the Global Financial Crisis of 2008–9, but still quite striking in light of a very low 4.5% unemployment rate in the US for most of 2016 and 2017. The concern has been decreasing since 2010, as shown in the Figure 10.1, but it still dominated people's concerns. Regardless of whether the fear is well placed or not, it does exist, and it pushes people to pay more attention to job security than to hours of work.

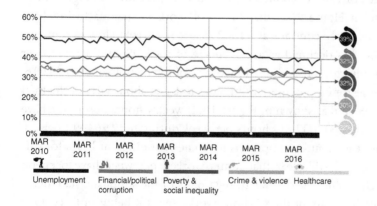

Figure 10.1 The World's Top Worries (in 25 Countries)

Source: www.weforum.org/agenda/2017/02/what-are-people-in-your-country-most-worried-about/.

Another issue raised in Figure 10.1 is concern about inequality, which was third on the list of worries. In an era when we hear constantly about the "other 99%" of people in the US (i.e., those not earning exorbitant incomes in the top 1% of US people[4]), there must be some importance to dividing up the economic pie more fairly. This is quite a challenge, and not one that the four-day workweek addresses.

REASONS WHY IT WILL WORK

The Existing Trajectory of Work Hours Over the Past Century

Even though the argument has been made here that the five-day, 40-hour workweek has been in place since 1926 in the US, this is a bit of an overstatement. As noted in Chapter 1, the average number of hours per week worked in the US since the end of the World War II has declined. According to the evidence presented by Aguiar and Hurst (2007), total work hours per week dropped from 51.6 hours in 1965 to 39.5 hours per week in 2003 for men, and rose from 22.5 hours in 1965 to 24.9 hours per week in 2003 for women. Women's non-market work (including work at home) declined from 32.9 hours per week to 22.6 hours per week over that period. Overall, people's amount of leisure time rose by about 3.7 hours per week from 1965 to 2003.

According to the US Bureau of Labor Statistics, the average number of hours worked in non-farm US employment went from about 38 hours per week in 1964 to about 34 hours in 1999, as shown in Figure 10.2.

Note in Figure 10.2 that hours of work in manufacturing have remained fairly constant at 41–42 hours per week. However, manufacturing has declined as a percentage of total US employment over these same years, reaching a low of 9% of total employment in 2016. Service sector employment dominates today, at about 90% of the total in the US. And as shown in Figure 10.2, weekly hours in services have declined to about 32–33 hours per week during the 1964–99 period.

From each source, despite using somewhat different bases for calculation, it is still clear that hours worked per week have been on the decline since World War II, regardless of the simplistic statements that one hears about the 40-hour workweek still being in force. One caveat to keep in mind is that the actual hours worked are less than a typically contracted 40 hours due to vacations, holidays, inclusion of part-time workers, and other elements that are counted in some of the

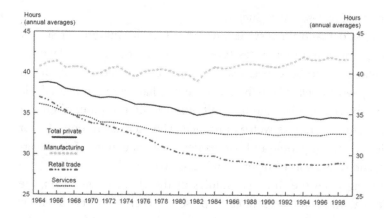

Figure 10.2 Average Weekly Hours for the Total Private Sector and Selected Industry Divisions, 1964–99

Source: Kirkland (2000, p. 29).

estimates. These complications often make it difficult to compare one measure to another, but the main point to note is that weekly work hours have been declining in all of the measures. So, moving to a 32-hour workweek would not be wildly out of line with the reality that already exists today.

There Actually Is Demand for a Shorter Workweek

While it is true that labor market pressures since World War II have focused mostly on job security and working conditions, there still is interest in reducing the workweek in a formal sense. That is, calls for a four-day, 32-hour workweek have come from labor groups as well as some (often high-tech) employers during this time period. And companies have found success in attracting workers into jobs offering a shorter workweek, as discussed in Chapter 3 above.

Just because organized labor is no longer as major a force in US labor relations as it used to be does not mean that labor's voice is not heard. Happily, what the decline of labor unions in the US means is a lower incidence of strikes and confrontations in labor–company relations. And at least in today's environment with less than 5% unemployment in the US, this means that employees have a reasonable degree of opportunity to switch employers when working conditions are not attractive.

153 **This Won't Work**

That is, as demand for services increases, it is driving greater supply of people working in services (even before the four-day workweek). This may seem to be a specious argument, but the fact is that once a four-day workweek is launched, people will have more time available for non-work activities, and this will produce some amount of greater demand for services as well as products. The increase in demand for services will spur people and companies to provide more of those services, and thus a sort of inverse Say's Law[5] will result.

Judging from the time use studies of the US in recent years, the additional time available once a person switches to the 32-hour workweek may be used to expand any number of activities, with the most logical ones being the ones in which the most time is already allocated – sleeping, watching TV, doing more household work, and leisure activities such as sports and arts.

CONCLUSIONS

It is certainly not possible to conclusively refute the naysayers concerning the four-day workweek. Since the proposed work arrangement is hypothetical, except in a small number of fairly isolated cases, it cannot be shown to have worked at this point. A very instructive empirical note is that the actual hours worked in the past half-century have definitely declined in the US, to an average that is not too far from 32 hours per week. So even without a concerted effort to pursue the four-day workweek goal, progress has been made toward that end. Formalizing the direction of work into the four-day, 32-hour basic structure is well within reach.

NOTES

1 It may be a small point, but if initial salaries/wages are kept at the same level as the year before the change to 32 hours per week, then the productivity gains for that year will help to reduce the cost to companies of maintaining salaries/wages at their existing levels.

2 Workers also could be supported by a program similar to Trade Adjustment Assistance, in which they would receive direct benefits for the fewer hours worked and subsidies for training to improve their job-related skills.

3 The World Economic Forum reported in 2017 that people's greatest fear was unemployment. This was followed by financial/political corruption, poverty, and social inequality. See www.weforum.org/agenda/2017/02/what-are-people-in-your-country-most-worried-about/.

4 See, for example, https://en.wikipedia.org/wiki/We_are_the_99%25.

5 Say's Law appeared originally in 1803 (Say, J.-B. [1834]. *A Treatise on Political Economy* (6th American ed.). Philadelphia, PA: Grigg & Elliott. This is an English translation of Say's *Traité d'Economie Politique*, published in 1803), and is briefly summarized in www.economicshelp.org/blog/glossary/says-law/.

REFERENCES

Aguiar, M. and E. Hurst (2007). "Measuring Trends in Leisure: The Allocation of Time over Five Decades". *Quarterly Journal of Economics*. Vol. 122, pp. 969–1006.

Kirkland, K. (2000). "On the Decline in Average Weekly Hours Worked", *Monthly Labor Review*. Vol. 123, pp. 26–31.

Tversky, A. and D. Kahneman (1974). "Judgment under Uncertainty: Heuristics and Biases". *Science*. Vol. 185, pp. 1124–1131.

Conclusions
Eleven

The arguments for the four-day workweek have been laid out and supported to the extent that this is possible. Since it is a counterfactual proposition – that is, we have not had such a labor arrangement previously – it is not possible to demonstrate empirically that it can and will function successfully. At the same time, we have experienced previous reductions in the workweek, particularly in the second half of the 19th century and during 1926–38, when most US businesses moved to a 40-hour, five-day workweek. The previous significant reductions from six 10–12-hour workdays to six eight-hour workdays and then to five eight-hour days per week occurred with much conflict between labor and employers and with some degree of government intervention. Happily, the same level of labor/company antagonism does not exist today, and the government in principle could step in with some supportive policy measures for the four-day, 32-hour workweek today.

The long history of the workweek shows even more emphatically that there is nothing sacred about a five-day, 40-hour workweek. In the 1800s, before the Civil War, workweeks typically were at least six days per week, with 10–12-hour workdays (from sunup to sundown). After the Civil War, labor union pressure and government policy were able to push the workweek down to about 60 hours per week from Monday through Saturday. Early in the 20th century, labor unions came to agreement with a number of companies to work a 48-hour workweek from Monday through Saturday. Most of these agreements happened just after World War I. Then came the eye-opening decision by Ford Motor Company in mid-1926 to operate a five-day, 40-hour workweek. This move was followed by a number of additional companies, until the Fair Labor Standards Act in 1938 established the 40-hour workweek for companies involved in inter-state commerce. Ford's policy was set almost 100 years ago. With technology advances

156 **Conclusions**

and income increases since then, it is more than appropriate to consider another downward shift in the workweek now.

A Brief Review of the Previous Ten Chapters

Next, some conclusions are presented that derive from each of the previous ten chapters in this book.

In Chapter 1, some of the evidence is presented concerning the US workweek in the 20th century, demonstrating that although the formal rule for working hours remains at about 40 hours per week, the reality is that average hours worked during the second half of the century declined at a slow but steady pace. Actual hours worked by people with full-time jobs at the beginning of the 21st century was about 39.5 hours for men and 24.9 hours for women. Women were found to work about ten hours per week more than men in "non-market work," including household work and caring for children. Data from the Bureau of Labor Statistics show that the average workweek for men and women combined in the US in June of 2017 was about 34.5 hours.[1]

This introductory chapter notes that possibly the greatest challenge to implementing a four-day workweek is people's resistance to change. If the workweek has been 40 hours over five days for almost 100 years, changing from this mental frame will be difficult. The naysayers will argue that working less time is evidence of slothful behavior – just as they did when the workweek dropped from 72 hours per week to 60 hours per week in the 1800s. They will say that it is impossible to live on less income, which may be part of the necessary start-up cost of the shorter week. This has not overwhelmed people in the limited cases where a shorter workweek was tried in the 20th century, but the examples are not numerous enough to provide unequivocal proof. Also, the logic of the four-day workweek calls for flexibility – for those people who need to work more hours for more income, the choice should remain open to them. Critics will probably find other arguments to oppose the four-day workweek, most of which will be due to the "framing" of the workweek at the current level and the inability to conceive of the new alternative in dispassionate, objective terms.

Chapter 2 looked at the quality of people's lives, measured in various ways from job satisfaction to overall life satisfaction to happiness indicators. It is asserted that the goal of working is to satisfy a number of objectives, beginning with earning enough income to live on.

Additional goals of working include satisfaction from interacting with other people, gaining a sense of power from work relationships, having opportunities to do interesting things, and achieving a sense of self-worth. The 32-hour workweek then needs to help people toward achieving overall life satisfaction, including both work goals and non-work goals.

The range of non-work goals goes from sleeping and eating to watching TV to exercising, obtaining further education, being involved in charitable activities, and more. Depending on each individual's preferences, the 32-hour workweek allows for greater pursuit of all of their non-work objectives – or use of the freed-up eight hours per week to work 40 hours as before. The key initial trade-off will be between slightly less income for working the shorter week and much greater opportunity to use that freed-up time as desired.[2]

A striking comparison of life satisfaction, job satisfaction, happiness, and other measures of people's views of their lives across multiple countries shows that the Nordic countries plus The Netherlands and Switzerland rank the highest (far above the US, which appears, in various rankings, from 12th to 23rd position). And if we compare the length of the workweek across countries, the five countries with the shortest workweeks in 2015 were The Netherlands, Denmark, Norway, Switzerland, and Germany. The US had the 23rd shortest average work-week among the 50 countries. The country measures of satisfaction versus length of the workweek were correlated at −63%, showing a strong tie between fewer work hours and greater satisfaction.

Chapter 3 looks at productivity and motivation in order to explore the likely outcome of reducing the workweek by one day. In previous cases of reducing the workweek, hourly productivity has jumped substantially. Henry Ford claimed that the number of cars produced once he dropped the workweek to 40 hours over five days instead of 48 hours over six days did not decline. That is, the productivity of the workers in his plants increased by approximately the same 17% that working time was reduced. It cannot be expected that precisely the same outcome will occur when moving from 40 hours to 32 hours per week, but it still should be true that motivation will improve and productivity will increase by some amount.

Chapter 4 looks in some detail at what people do with their time during the week beyond working. Of course, sleeping is a major activity, averaging about eight hours per day for Americans through the years. The other activities beyond work include doing housework, watching TV, entertainment other than TV, and a wide variety of additional activities such as education, sports, arts, and charitable endeavors. The logic of the four-day workweek is that people would spend more of their time on non-work activities. And if we look at typical weekend activities today, they parallel weekday activities, with much more time spent on things like sleeping, watching TV, finding other entertainment, and housework during non-work days.

An interesting implication of the extra weekend day is that companies and individuals would have to provide more of the goods and services used in the non-work activities. From more television sets and more TV programming, to more goods and services for home care, to more national and state parks and more clothing for outdoor activities, the range of additional production will be cause for greater employment in producing those things.

Chapter 5 considers the question of who will pay for the shorter workweek. It is expected that increased productivity resulting from the fewer hours worked will balance out part of the 20% reduction in weekly work hours. Beyond that, assuming that increased productivity does not just completely equal the lost hours, somebody has to pay. If workers keep their same incomes, then companies would pay. If workers lost 20% of their incomes, this would obviously be a huge hit to their ability to pay the bills. If greater productivity cancelled out part of the lost hours, then the resulting difference would still need to be split somehow. Chapter 5 looks at various alternatives, including a government subsidy (paid for by all taxpayers) that would help families and/or companies with tax deductions or other tax shields to increase after-tax income.

This challenge may be the greatest one to deal with in converting to a four-day, 32-hour workweek. Whatever other issues arise, people need income to survive, and they will be resistant to losses in that income, even if they are only temporary. A productivity increase is sure to accompany the reduced work hours, but the size of that increase is not at all clear beforehand, and it will certainly differ across jobs.

Chapter 6 considers the challenge of automation/mechanization of work through machines. This concern has existed since the dawn of the Industrial Revolution, and consistently through the decades and centuries more jobs have resulted from greater movement of people from physical labor to knowledge labor. It is not clear exactly what jobs will provide the most opportunities in the future, but it is very clear that they will not be in agriculture or in traditional manufacturing.

In the current context of globalized production, it appears that for people in the US, the best kinds of jobs will be ones that require problem-solving ability and creativity that machines cannot match, plus ones that are services that require human skill such as food preparation, facilities maintenance, haircutting, and in-person health assistance. These jobs fall at two ends of the income distribution; people who are in the middle-income range face the greatest challenge of possibly being replaced by machines in the future.

Chapter 7 goes to the detail of how a four-day workweek would be implemented. When some services are not offered any longer on Fridays, how will people's needs be served? If your work is managerial or professional, how will you be able to move to a four-day workweek? In elementary and secondary education, how will school weeks be able to operate on a four-day workweek calendar? Each of these questions and many more are discussed in Chapter 7, and possible solutions are offered. The fundamental principle is that the four-day workweek has to have another day added to the weekend, presumably either Friday or Monday. This would enable everyone to operate on a similar basis. Jobs and businesses that provide service or production during the entire week and/or for long hours each day, such as hotels, restaurants, and some retail stores, will just have to add staffing to cover the hours that are freed up when individual employees reduce their work hours to 32 per week. Chapter 7 also provides a numerical example to demonstrate the manageability of this task.

Chapter 8 presents a history of the workweek since the early days of the Industrial Revolution. Not surprisingly by this point in the discussion, working hours have declined over time, mainly due to mechanization of work activities and also due to the shift from agriculture as the main sector of employment to services filling that role. Manufacturing has never been the largest of the three sectors, but it declined persistently in the second half of the 20th century to where today it accounts for just about 10% of US jobs. Historically, manufacturing jobs had the longest hours for workers (not necessarily for managers), but those have declined to a similar level as for service workers in the 21st century. Over the decades and centuries, the length of the workweek has decreased, not due to specific crises or obvious turning points, but rather to evolving conditions (mainly technology changes) that have enabled people to move to the shorter working time.

The reasons why the workweek became the center of attention for companies in the late 1800s were pressure from organized labor to reduce the heavy burden of long hours and also pressure from government to likewise reduce the burden on people working 60- or 70-hour weeks. This pressure resurfaced after World War I, and companies largely moved to a six-day, 48-hour workweek at that time. Ford's monumental shift to a five-day, 40-hour workweek soon followed in 1926. After that, for just about 100 years, we have had no formal reduction in the workweek in the US. There have been moves to try a four-day, 40-hour workweek, to offer more flexible work hours, and to allow people to work remotely from the office or factory, but no large-scale change has occurred in this past century, except perhaps for a large increase in part-time work.

Chapter 9 projects the workweek and the workplace into the future, considering arrangements such as working from home, having a flexible schedule, shifting more to contract work rather than employee–employer structures, and other ideas. While all of these innovations have changed the face of work for a number of people, still the vast majority work five-day weeks at the workplace. Even so, about a third of people today are able to work remotely for at least part of the week, and about 10% have some degree of flexibility in their hours. Those working in the "gig economy," such as people working for Uber or Airbnb, constituted less than 1% of total US employment in 2016.

While there are surely some trends underway that will alter the employment landscape another 30 or 40 years from now, there is not a clear pattern of change other than schedule flexibility and the increase in the opportunity to work from remote locations rather than at the office/factory. The fact that the average time with the current employer was 5.0 years in 1983 and has changed to 5.1 years in 2016 does not indicate any noticeable change in habits of the millennials versus the baby boomers. (However, if we look at just the age bracket of people from 25–34 years old, the change was in the other direction – from an average of 3.0 years with the current employer in 1983 to 2.8 years in 2016.) Most likely the key reasons for this less-than-overwhelming shift to alternative work arrangements are: (1) the lack of job security; and (2) the lack of health insurance in many of these arrangements.

Chapter 10 returns to the challenge posed by the naysayers: this won't work! The arguments that they raise, from reduced incomes to moving away from the current framing of the workweek as being 40 hours, are tackled one by one. One clear piece of evidence is that the actual week worked by people in the US has declined over the past half-century, to where in June 2017 the average time actually worked per week by Americans is about 34.5 hours. This is to some extent due to part-time work, mostly chosen by people and not forced on them, and this number of hours demonstrates that the shorter workweek is entirely possible, even in a "workaholic" environment such as the US. The challenge is to break the current mind-set or anchoring of people's views concerning the workweek, to escape the mental box that says that we work 40 hours per week over five days (or more for managerial/professional people).

Summarizing many of the points raised in this book, an overview of the issues is shown in Table 11.1.

It is clear that the *potential* benefits in terms of well-being or "happiness" by reducing the standard workweek from 40 hours to 32 hours via the four-day workweek outweigh the expected costs. The largest challenge to making such a stepwise change in working conditions is likely to be people's psychological resistance to working less and therefore feeling less valuable or less important, as well as initially having less income. Working hours have been on a declining trend for about 200 years, so this would not be an unusual or unsustainable situation. And it should be re-emphasized: for those who do not wish to take advantage of the shorter workweek, the opportunity must remain to work "overtime" to get back to the 40 hours (or more) that some people prefer to work. After several years, the societal norm would be established at 32 hours per week, and then people would "anchor" their expectations on this basis, so it would be easier for them to accept that load.

Leadership to see this change become a reality is needed from the heads of major companies, who can lead both by statements in

Table 11.1 Pros and Cons of the Four-Day Workweek

Pros	Cons
Increases time for leisure, charity, education, and other activities	Requires individuals to deal with initially reduced incomes for reduced work time
Related to the point above: increases happiness, satisfaction, and/or well-being of the population	Not feasible in all employment categories
Also related to the points above: work productivity increases due to greater job satisfaction and to fewer hours at work	Increases the number of days per week without service availability from businesses closed three days per week
Historical evidence shows that reduced work hours have not reduced national output	Dealing with the reduced output per person will require companies to cope with compensation issues and a greater number of employees
Reduces commuting costs for individuals	
Increases job opportunities for those who fill in for the 20% of reduced work time, despite mechanization of some existing jobs	The adjustment period will bring about friction as some businesses move quickly to 32 hours and others don't

support of this change and also by demonstration with their own companies' working hours. If a group such as the Conference Board member companies, the major auto manufacturers and banks, or the Fortune 100 were to take this bold step, it certainly would spread through the workforce quickly. Examples of a flexible workweek at tech companies such as Google and Facebook, as well as Virgin and Amazon.com, may also help in getting the change underway. Moving from the inertia that has existed since the 1920s into this new framework is the key challenge.

In the 32-hour workweek, there is a disruptive change in working conditions, with offices presumably only open four days per week. This is noteworthy, and it is different for office workers relative to retail store employees and others whose businesses are not closed after the regular workdays and on weekends. So there may be something of a devil in the details of how individuals will be treated in this new system, and this will have to be worked out, as suggested partially in the pages above.

Maybe a new (weekend) day will be dawning soon.[3]

NOTES

1 See Bureau of Labor Statistics website: www.bls.gov/news.release/empsit.t18.htm.
2 As shown in Chapter 5, people would probably have an income reduction of about 10%, assuming an increase in hourly productivity with the shorter workweek, so either that salary reduction could be accepted in exchange for greater free time or the person could work about four hours above the 32 hours per week to recoup lost income.
3 At what point should we sit back and think about the question: how much of our lives should be dedicated to working for income and how much should be allocated to other activities (leisure, charity, education, etc.)? This is not just an existential question; company leaders will have to be the ones who make the decision of whether we choose to move to a shorter workweek.

Index